WHERE TO MAKE MONEY

WHERE TO MAKE MONEY

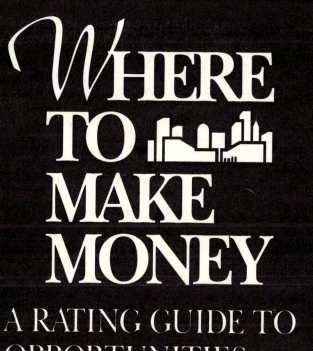

A RATING GUIDE TO OPPORTUNITIES IN AMERICA'S METRO AREAS

- Business
- Employment
- Economic Momentum
- Women & Minorities
- Growth Potential
- Real Estate

G. SCOTT THOMAS

PROMETHEUS BOOKS • BUFFALO, NEW YORK

Published 1993 by Prometheus Books

97 96 95 94 93   5 4 3 2 1

Library of Congress Cataloging-in-Publication Data

Thomas, G. Scott.
    Where to make money : a rating guide to opportunities in America's metro areas / G. Scott Thomas.
        p.   cm.
    ISBN 0-87975-762-0 (cloth)
    ISBN 0-87975-795-7 (paper)
    1. Cities and towns—United States—Ratings. 2. Cities and towns—United States—Statistics. 3. Metropolitan areas—United States—Statistics. 4. Labor market—United States—Statistics. 5. New business enterprises—United States—Statistics. I. Title.
HT123.T45   1993
307.76'0973—dc20   92-37008
                                                                                   CIP

Portions of this book previously appeared in a different form in *Biz, Business First,* and *American Demographics,* September 1991. Copyright © *American Demographics.* Reprinted with permission.

Printed on acid-free paper in the United States of America.

Contents

Introduction:

The
Importance
of Where

Newspaper reporters have a useful system that prompts them to record all the essential facts of a breaking story. Every beginning journalism student learns how to use this system, but even the canniest veteran relies on it every day. It is a series of one-word questions known collectively as the five W's, which is a bit misleading, since it actually is five W's and an H. But more about that in a moment.

The reporter can take a quick tour through the highlights of a story by using the five W's. The system is particularly helpful when a deadline is just minutes away and the editor is waiting impatiently for results. It works this way:

Who? Neil Armstrong.
What? Was the first person to walk on the moon.
Where? The moon's Sea of Tranquillity.

8

When? July 20, 1969.

Why? President Kennedy had pledged in 1961 that the United States would put a man on the moon before the end of the 1960s.

How? An accelerated $56 billion program developed the technology to shuttle Armstrong and his Apollo 11 crewmates to the moon and back.

It's really very simple. String together the five W's and you have what reporters call a lead, the capsule of important facts that begins any newspaper story. Then you can finish the job by filling underneath the lead with further details, quotes, and observations.

The usefulness of the five W's is not limited to journalism. This system also can be helpful in everyday life, clearing away the distractions that prevent you from analyzing your personal situation. It can, for example, clarify your thoughts about the way you make a living:

Who? You.

What? Are a bank vice president.

When? You have worked for the bank ever since 1977; you have been vice president since 1990.

Why? Banking seemed like interesting work when you were a college student. It is not nearly so interesting now that you've been in it for years, but it's the field that you know best. What the heck, it's a living.

How? You earned a bachelor's degree in economics. Then you worked your way up in the bank from loan officer to branch manager to various administrative posts, finally leading to the vice presidency.

You will notice that we left out one of the five W's, a question that in many respects is the most important of all:

Where?

The immediate answer is Chicago or Cheyenne, Wyoming, or Sheboygan Falls, Wisconsin—wherever you currently work. But this book is designed to make you think about this W in the future tense: *Where* can you earn the best living in coming years? *Where* can you find the area that will offer you the best chance to make money?

Let's return momentarily to the present to ponder something easier: Why do you live where you do?

No doubt you have many good reasons. Perhaps this is where you have always lived; it's where your extended family is. That's an important point. Perhaps you like the weather or the schools or the health-care system or any of a hundred other things. Those all are important, too.

But this book is about the one consideration that you might be ignoring—indeed, that millions of people *do* ignore—a consideration that is particularly worthy of your attention in these tough financial times: *Where* is the place that will provide you with the best possible economic opportunities? Is it your hometown, or is it somewhere else?

Your immediate reaction might be that things are fine as they are. Sure, you would love to make more money, but you really can't complain. Your hometown is like any place else. People have careers; some run their own businesses; some own nice homes. What could you possibly do elsewhere that you can't do right here?

Fair question. It's true that all communities offer economic opportunities to some people. Every city and town has a bank president, a wealthy real estate developer, and a prosperous store owner. They definitely have found the place that makes economic sense for them.

Can you match their success? Your education and skills and experience will have much to say about that. But it's a fact that your odds of success vary greatly from place to place across the country, regardless of your education and skills and experience. Some areas are expanding economically, creating opportunities for large numbers of people; others are virtually stagnant, making it very difficult to get ahead.

The experts know that this is the case. Just ask Jon Goodman, director of the entrepreneur program at the University of Southern California.

"Where you live is extremely important," says Goodman. "It's a function of that old marketing saw. You know, the one about the three components of a successful business: location, location, location."

Or ask Nestor Terleckyj, president of NPA Data Services, a Washington demographics firm, whether your choice of a hometown can affect your chances of making a good living.

"It matters a great deal," he says. "If you're stuck in a place where a military base closes, let's say, you're in trouble. Even a dentist could lose a lot of business. Almost everybody is affected."

It stands to reason that Terleckyj's observation is universally true. Almost everybody is affected by any major swing in an area's economic health. The doors to advancement swing open if a place is steadily creating businesses and jobs, but there are awesome barriers to personal progress if an area's employment base is slowly eroding.

This is nothing new. Americans always have understood the importance of *where.*

• It was the reason that Europeans colonized this continent. They wanted to start over in a new world that did not suffer from Europe's overpopulation, stifling class system, and excessive reverence for tradition.

• It was the reason that Horace Greeley advised all young men to go west and grow up with the country. The pioneers headed west, always west, seeking fertile farmland or dreaming of gold.

• It is the reason that millions of us move in the course of a year,

10 clutching to the hope that each new town will be the place that makes a dramatic, permanent difference in our lives. Americans are so mobile that fewer than 40 percent of the residents of many Southern and Western cities are natives of the states in which they now live.

Yes, there is an element of wishful thinking in our search for the perfect hometown. But there also is a large element of realism. Where you live *does* make a difference in your paycheck and your bank account. It *does* help determine what type of job you have, whether you can start your own business, and how easily you can invest in real estate. Why do you think we always talk about being in the right *place* at the right time?

This book is designed to help you find that place. It uses the latest official statistics to rate the economic opportunities available in the nation's major metropolitan areas. You will learn the best places to find a job, start a business, and buy real estate, as well as the areas that are most likely to grow in the future and are most willing to help women and minorities advance in the present.

The results of these separate categories are added together in the second chapter, yielding an overall ranking of all areas in the order of their economic health. The third chapter contains detailed report cards that provide additional information to help you find the area that is best for you, the place that will give you the best chance to make money.

We will begin that search in a few pages. First there are a few things you should know about the geographic areas included in this book and some of the terms that you will encounter.

Metropolitan Areas

America still is a country of wide open spaces. The landscape from Atlantic to Pacific features broad expanses of farmland, seemingly endless plains, dense forests, vast deserts, imposing mountain ranges, and thousands upon thousands of rivers and lakes.

But that is not the America that most of us know. We don't live isolated in forests or in the middle of deserts or on mountain peaks. We live in cities and suburbs; we are at home in the urban sprawls known as metropolitan areas.

We certainly are not alone. The U.S. Census Bureau, which is precise about such things, reports that 192,725,741 people resided in the nation's 284 metropolitan areas in 1990. That works out to 77.5 percent of the entire country, almost eight of every ten Americans.

And those numbers are increasing every day. Metro areas added 20 million people during the 1980s, a population increase of 11.6 percent. All the rest of the country—what we call nonmetropolitan America—grew by **11** only 2.1 million people, or 3.9 percent, in the same decade.

Most of us obviously have decided that our futures lie in large cities and their suburbs. That's why this book focuses on the economic opportunities to be found in metro areas.

But we don't have enough space here to deal extensively with all 284 metros, an unwieldy group. And let's be honest: The federal government has given the metropolitan designation to some areas that are decidedly unmetropolitan, places like Grand Forks, North Dakota; Casper, Wyoming; and Enid, Oklahoma.

This book, therefore, will concentrate on areas that have at least 500,000 residents. There are 73 of these major metropolitan areas, ranging in size from New York City (17,953,372 residents) to Charleston, South Carolina (506,875). We will confine our attention to this group for three reasons:

1. Fully 60 percent of all Americans live in the 73 major metros, which have a total of 149 million residents. That also works out to more than three-quarters of the combined population of all 284 metros.

2. Major metropolitan areas are instantly recognizable. You might not be able to match state names with metro areas such as Pine Bluff, Kankakee, and Victoria. (Answers: Arkansas, Illinois, and Texas.) But everyone knows where to find Little Rock, Chicago, and Dallas.

3. Major metros are regional economic centers. Many are banking, distribution, and employment hubs for entire states or sections of the country.

Each metropolitan area consists of cities and suburbs that are "socially and economically interrelated," as determined by the U.S. Office of Management and Budget. Some metros, such as Bakersfield and El Paso, are limited to a single county. Others are quite extensive. The New York City area is spread across 24 counties in three states; metropolitan Atlanta covers 18 counties in Georgia.

This book uses the metropolitan boundaries established by the federal government, but we'll try to be less formal about it. Take the very first area on our list as an example. The government has given it a grandiose (and very bureaucratic) name: the Albany-Schenectady-Troy Metropolitan Statistical Area. Gives you a nice homey feeling, doesn't it? We'll just call it the Albany metro area. Different names, same thing.

One last point: Keep in mind that this book is focused broadly on metropolitan areas, not narrowly on central cities. When we mention Chicago or Grand Rapids or Jacksonville, we are referring to the entire Chicago or Grand Rapids or Jacksonville metro areas—central cities, suburbs, the whole bit. In the rare case that we want to talk specifically about a city, we will make the distinction clear.

Metro Area	Main State (Other States)	Number of Counties	Population
Albany	New York	6	874,304
Allentown	Pennsylvania (New Jersey)	4	686,688
Atlanta	Georgia	18	2,833,511
Austin	Texas	3	781,572
Bakersfield	California	1	543,477
Baltimore	Maryland	7*	2,382,172
Baton Rouge	Louisiana	4	528,264
Birmingham	Alabama	5	907,810
Boston	Massachusetts	5	3,783,817
Buffalo	New York	2	1,189,288
Charleston	South Carolina	3	506,875
Charlotte	North Carolina (South Carolina)	7	1,162,093
Chicago	Illinois (Indiana, Wisconsin)	11	8,065,633
Cincinnati	Ohio (Indiana, Kentucky)	8	1,744,124
Cleveland	Ohio	7	2,759,823
Columbus	Ohio	7	1,377,419
Dallas	Texas	9	3,885,415
Dayton	Ohio	4	951,270
Denver	Colorado	6	1,848,319
Detroit	Michigan	8	4,665,236
El Paso	Texas	1	591,610
Fresno	California	1	667,490
Grand Rapids	Michigan	2	688,399
Greensboro	North Carolina	7	942,091
Greenville	South Carolina	3	640,861
Harrisburg	Pennsylvania	4	587,986
Hartford	Connecticut	3	1,123,678

* includes independent cities

Metro Area	Main State (Other States)	Number of Counties	Population
Honolulu	Hawaii	1	836,231
Houston	Texas	7	3,711,043
Indianapolis	Indiana	8	1,249,822
Jacksonville	Florida	4	906,727
Kansas City	Missouri (Kansas)	10	1,566,280
Knoxville	Tennessee	7	604,816
Las Vegas	Nevada	1	741,459
Little Rock	Arkansas	4	513,117
Los Angeles	California	5	14,531,529
Louisville	Kentucky (Indiana)	7	952,662
Memphis	Tennessee (Arkansas, Mississippi)	4	981,747
Miami	Florida	2	3,192,582
Milwaukee	Wisconsin	5	1,607,183
Minneapolis	Minnesota (Wisconsin)	11	2,464,124
Nashville	Tennessee	8	985,026
New Haven	Connecticut	1	804,219
New Orleans	Louisiana	6	1,238,816
New York City	New York (Connecticut, New Jersey)	24	17,953,372
Norfolk	Virginia	12*	1,396,107
Oklahoma City	Oklahoma	6	958,839
Omaha	Nebraska (Iowa)	4	618,262
Orlando	Florida	3	1,072,748
Philadelphia	Pennsylvania (Delaware, Maryland, New Jersey)	13	5,899,345
Phoenix	Arizona	1	2,122,101
Pittsburgh	Pennsylvania	5	2,242,798
Portland	Oregon (Washington)	5	1,477,895
Providence	Rhode Island	4	916,270
Raleigh	North Carolina	4	735,480

Metro Area	Main State (Other States)	Number of Counties	Population
Richmond	Virginia	13*	865,640
Rochester	New York	5	1,002,410
Sacramento	California	4	1,481,102
Saint Louis	Missouri (Illinois)	10*	2,444,099
Salt Lake City	Utah	3	1,072,227
San Antonio	Texas	3	1,302,099
San Diego	California	1	2,498,016
San Francisco	California	10	6,253,311
Scranton	Pennsylvania	5	734,175
Seattle	Washington	3	2,559,164
Springfield	Massachusetts	2	602,878
Syracuse	New York	3	659,864
Tampa	Florida	4	2,067,959
Toledo	Ohio	3	614,128
Tucson	Arizona	1	666,880
Tulsa	Oklahoma	5	708,954
Washington	District of Columbia (Maryland, Virginia)	16*	3,923,574
West Palm Beach	Florida	1	863,518

Glossary of Important Terms

Demographic, geographic, and statistical terms used in this book are defined in the glossary below. You might consider some of the terms to be self-explanatory, and you will find a few that also are defined elsewhere in the book. But all have been collected here for easy reference.

East. One of the four major regions in the country. It includes Connecticut, Delaware, the District of Columbia, Maine, Maryland, Massachusetts, New Hampshire, New Jersey, New York, Pennsylvania, Rhode Island, Vermont, and West Virginia.

Great Lakes area. A sub-region that consists of states from the East and the Midwest. It includes Illinois, Indiana, Michigan, Minnesota, New York, Ohio, Pennsylvania, and Wisconsin.

Major metropolitan area. A metro area that has a population of more than 500,000. There are 73 major metros.

Median. The middle number in a group when all figures are arranged according to size. Don't confuse *median* with *average*. Let's say that three communities have 428, 326, and 125 manufacturing plants respectively. The median number is 326, while the average is 293.

Metro center. The dominant city in a metropolitan area. (This book names each metro area after its metro center.)

16 **Metropolitan area.** A large city and its suburbs, or a combination of neighboring large cities and their suburbs, that are defined by the federal government as "socially and economically interrelated." There are 284 of these areas. Also called *metro area* or *metro*.

Midwest. One of the nation's four major regions. It includes Illinois, Indiana, Iowa, Kansas, Michigan, Minnesota, Missouri, Nebraska, North Dakota, Ohio, South Dakota, and Wisconsin.

New England. A sub-region of the East that includes Connecticut, Maine, Massachusetts, New Hampshire, Rhode Island, and Vermont.

Per capita. A rate expressed per each person living in an area. A per capita figure is calculated by taking any total number for the area (e.g., the number of fire trucks, restaurants, or retail outlets) and dividing it by the area's population. Let's say that a city has 20,000 residents who earn a total of $600 million a year. That is $30,000 per capita.

Rates. It often is unfair to compare absolute totals from two metros of different sizes, so the totals are projected to a common rate to put both areas on an equal footing. Consider this example: Metro A has 2,500 police officers and a population of 550,000; Metro B has 1,600 officers and a population of 300,000. Rates are commonly, though not always, expressed as a number per 100,000 residents. Metro A has 455 officers per 100,000 residents; Metro B has 533 per 100,000.

South. One of the nation's four major regions. It includes Alabama, Arkansas, Florida, Georgia, Kentucky, Louisiana, Mississippi, North Carolina, Oklahoma, South Carolina, Tennessee, Texas, and Virginia.

Southwest. A sub-region that consists of states from the South and the West. It includes Arizona, New Mexico, Oklahoma, and Texas.

West. One of the nation's four major regions. It includes Alaska, Arizona, California, Colorado, Hawaii, Idaho, Montana, Nevada, New Mexico, Oregon, Utah, Washington, and Wyoming.

1

The Tests

L et's start by being honest. You probably picked up this book because the title caught your eye. You would like to know, quite frankly, *where to make money.* There is just one simple question on your mind: Which metropolitan areas in the United States offer the best economic opportunities?

Unfortunately, there is no simple answer. Or at least there is no answer that can be easily arrived at. Several factors affect the quality of a given metro area's economic climate; six are of particular importance. We must take a careful look at each of these factors before handing down a final verdict.

So we'll begin not with answers, but with questions of our own. The ideal metro area—if such a place exists—would be able to answer yes to all of the following:

1. Did the area gather *economic momentum* in the 1980s? Did it register strong increases in population and per capita income during the decade?

2. Does the area have the potential for *future growth*? Will it continue to expand at an impressive pace through the 1990s and well into the next century? Does it have enough space to easily accommodate this additional expansion?

3. Does the metro offer a large number of *job opportunities*? Does

18 it have a rapidly expanding job base, coupled with a low unemployment rate?

4. Does the area abound with *business opportunities*? Does it encourage the establishment of new businesses, particularly in the retail and service sectors?

5. Does the metro have a substantial number of affordable *real estate opportunities*? Is its housing stock reasonably priced? Are its property taxes low?

6. Does the area offer *equality of opportunities*? Does it extend the same chances to all people, regardless of gender or race?

These questions, as you certainly have noticed, have been carefully arranged into six groups, each with a phrase in italics. This chapter consists of six statistical tests that will supply the answers to these questions. The key phrases above are the names of the tests.

We will measure the performances of all 73 major metro areas in all six categories. The results of these tests will identify each area's strengths and weaknesses, and also will help us determine where the best overall economic opportunities can be found.

We have a couple of housekeeping matters to address before getting down to this work. The next two subheadings explain how the tests are put together and where all of the statistics come from. You can skip ahead if you're not particularly interested in the fine print. Head straight to Test No. 1: Economic Momentum.

Scoring

All six tests are set up in exactly the same way. Let's check out the structure, point by point, using the economic momentum test as an example:

Components. Each test has two components. They count equally toward the final test score; it's a 50–50 split. The two components of the economic momentum test are population growth and per capita income growth.

Component scoring. A metro area's score on a component is a reflection of the area's relative standing in that category. The score is expressed on a 100-point scale. The closer the area is to the top performance in the country, the higher its score is.

The extreme ends of the population growth component are Las Vegas, which grew 60.1 percent during the 1980s, and Pittsburgh, which lost 7.4 percent. The range between Las Vegas and Pittsburgh is 67.5 percentage points. (Las Vegas automatically earns 100 points. Pittsburgh, naturally enough, gets none.)

Raleigh registered population growth of 31.2 percent from 1980 to

1990, earning 57 points. Here's how the math works: Raleigh's growth rate is 38.6 percentage points higher than Pittsburgh's. Divide 38.6 into the total range (67.5), and you get 57 percent.

An exception. There are a few components in which the top area performs much better than all other metros. The first-place and second-place areas both are awarded 100 points in any case where the difference between the two areas is more than 10 percent. The scores for the other areas are figured in relation to the performance of the second-place metro, not the top one. This is done to prevent a single component from distorting the total scores on any test.

The same procedure is followed in reverse if the last-place area is more than 10 percent worse than the next-to-last metro; both areas get no points in such a case. Check out the woman-owned businesses component for an example; both the top and bottom of the list have been handled this way.

Test scoring. This is easy. Add the two component scores and divide by two. (Round upward if the average ends in a decimal.) Raleigh received 57 points for population growth and 81 for per capita income growth. That yields a final score of 69 points on the economic momentum test.

The curve. All grading in this book is done on the curve. Letter grades are awarded according to the following scale, though slight deviations are dictated by natural breaks in a few cases.

A This grade is given to the top 10 percent of the 73 metros, which works out to seven areas.
B The next 25 percent, or 18 areas.
C The next 45 percent, or 33 areas.
D The next 15 percent, or 11 areas.
F The bottom 5 percent, or four areas.

Raleigh, with a score of 69 points, ranks fifth on the economic momentum test. That puts it safely in the top 10 percent, earning a grade of A.

Metro areas at the top of each grade level are given pluses (+), while those at the bottom are given minuses (–). But only one A+ is awarded on each test; it is reserved for the area with the highest score.

Sources

All statistics in this book are from recent government reports. Some charts on the following pages contain numbers that were transcribed straight from official sources. Other charts have figures that were generated specifically for this book; government statistics were used in those calculations.

20   Below is a complete bibliography, including capsule summaries of the information available from each source:

U.S. Bureau of the Census. *Census of Governments: Compendium of Government Finances.* Washington, D.C.: U.S. Government Printing Office, 1989. Includes property tax rates for all counties.

U.S. Bureau of the Census. *Census of Population.* Washington, D.C.: U.S. Government Printing Office, 1991–1992. The ultimate source. Has population and housing statistics for every locality from the smallest town to the biggest metro.

U.S. Bureau of the Census. *County and City Data Book.* Washington, D.C.: U.S. Government Printing Office, 1988. Is a source of census figures from throughout the 1980s. Also has maps that show the precise boundaries of all metropolitan areas.

U.S. Bureau of the Census. *County Business Patterns.* Washington, D.C.: U.S. Government Printing Office, 1991. Has county-by-county statistics on businesses and workers in all employment sectors.

U.S. Bureau of the Census. "Half of the Nation's Population Lives in Large Metropolitan Areas." Press release (February 21, 1991). Includes a complete listing of the nation's metro areas in order of population.

U.S. Bureau of the Census. *State and Metropolitan Area Data Book.* Washington, D.C.: U.S. Government Printing Office, 1991. Has pages of statistics for each metro area, including detailed employment and salary figures.

U.S. Bureau of the Census. *Survey of Minority-Owned Business Enterprises.* Washington, D.C.: U.S. Government Printing Office, 1991. Counts the number of businesses owned by minority-group members in each metro area.

U.S. Bureau of the Census. *Women-Owned Businesses.* Washington, D.C.: U.S. Government Printing Office, 1990. Provides area-by-area statistics on companies owned by women.

U.S. Bureau of Economic Analysis. *Regional Projections to 2040.* Washington, D.C.: U.S. Government Printing Office, 1990. Contains population and employment estimates for all of the nation's metro areas during the coming half-century.

U.S. Bureau of Economic Analysis. *Survey of Current Business,* volumes 66 (April 1986) and 71 (April 1991). Includes per capita income figures for all counties and metro areas.

U.S. Bureau of Labor Statistics. *Employment and Earnings,* volumes 34 (May 1987), 36 (May 1989), and 38 (May 1991). Has annual employment statistics for each metro area, including unemployment rates and total numbers of jobs.

Test No. 1: Economic Momentum

Las Vegas was a fairly insignificant desert community when Frank Mac-Donald's family moved there from Niagara Falls, New York, shortly after the end of World War II. Still in the future were the things for which the city now is famous: miles of massive casinos and the explosion of neon known as the Strip.

"It was nothing like it is now," MacDonald says. "Las Vegas was more like a small town. Things were just starting to happen."

The pre-war census in 1940 counted only 8,400 people in Las Vegas. MacDonald, now the state labor commissioner of Nevada, has seen the desert bloom into a metro area with a population of 741,000 in 1990.

"Las Vegas just keeps growing," he says. "The latest thing is they're building a number of very large resort hotels. Some of these places are essentially theme parks on a par with Disneyland. As you might expect, construction is growing by leaps and bounds."

And so, as a result, is Las Vegas. The metro area's population increased by 278,000 people during the 1980s alone, a gain of 60.1 percent. The rapid pace of this expansion earned Las Vegas the nation's top score for population growth, the first component of the economic momentum test.

Las Vegas and the two runners-up from Florida on the population growth list, Orlando and West Palm Beach, have similar profiles. All three are warm-weather metros that are broadly attractive to tourists, retirees, and young people looking for jobs. Orlando expanded by 53.3 percent between 1980 and 1990, while West Palm Beach grew by 49.7 percent.

"The 1980s were a perfect setup for Florida to move ahead, and it did," says Carol Taylor West, an economic forecaster at the University of Florida. "The bottom end of the baby boom generation was still moving into the labor pool, and many of them came to Florida for work. Population growth and job growth interacted to accelerate in a positive direction."

A substantial number of those young job-seekers hailed from the old industrial cities around the Great Lakes. These Rustbelt communities suffered throughout the 1980s as their manufacturing sectors weakened. The Pittsburgh area lost 7.4 percent of its population over the decade, the biggest decline in the country. Buffalo, Cleveland, Detroit, and Toledo also had fewer residents in 1990 than in 1980.

"I think you could lump northeast Ohio [Cleveland] in the same region with western New York [Buffalo] and western Pennsylvania [Pittsburgh]," says James Kell, business and industry manager of the Ohio Data Users Center in Columbus. "A lot of the forces working against them were similar. That whole area was hit by a decline in durable-goods manufacturing, particularly in the early 1980s."

22   But the Rustbelt was an exception to the prosperity that blanketed much of the nation during the latter half of the 1980s. Those same years brought high-octane economic expansion to the Atlantic Seaboard, where companies in the finance, insurance, and real estate sector seemed to set new profit records annually.

The business boom in the East was reflected in bank accounts and paychecks. Per capita income increased by 49.4 percent in Baltimore and New York City between 1984 and 1989, giving those two areas the nation's highest scores for income growth, the second component of this test. Boston, Hartford, and Springfield were close behind.

"A lot of it was tied to an overheated economy," recalls Paul Getman, managing director of Regional Financial Associates, a forecasting firm in West Chester, Pennsylvania. "The whole Northeast exploded in a construction boom. It seemed like there was a new office building on every block. But it was just a bubble, a bubble that later burst."

They know all about bursting bubbles in the oil belt that stretches from the Gulf of Mexico to the dry plains of the Southwest. A sharp drop in petroleum prices triggered the infamous energy bust of the mid-1980s. Unemployment skyrocketed across the region, reaching double-digit percentages in Houston and New Orleans.

Many of those who still had jobs found themselves limited to tiny raises or placed under wage freezes. It is no surprise that of the ten metro areas with the smallest income growth between 1984 and 1989, nine relied significantly on energy industries. At the bottom of the list was Oklahoma City, where per capita income grew by only 17.7 percent over the period.

"The oil bust hit us so hard. It was a big-time downturn," says Jeff Wallace, coordinator of the Oklahoma State Data Center. "But it also opened everybody's eyes. In the '70s and '80s, I don't want to say we were totally oil-based, but it was the majority [of the economy]. Now we're a lot more into manufacturing and services. If it hit us again, we'd be in a much better position to handle it."

The A+ metro area for economic momentum. Las Vegas emerged from the 1980s with incredible vigor, earning the area the top score on this test. It led the nation in population growth between 1980 and 1990, and it ranked seventh in income growth. Per capita income expanded by a robust 45 percent in the Las Vegas area from 1984 to 1989.

"The latter half of the decade was when things really got moving," says Jeff Hardcastle, a planning official for Clark County, Nevada, which includes Las Vegas. "We had a couple of fairly large casinos open, with more on the way. They're a steady source of construction jobs, along with all of the jobs at the casinos themselves. When you have an increasing job base like ours, it just draws people in."

Las Vegas led a Sunbelt sweep of the A range on this test. West Palm **23**
Beach, Orlando, Sacramento, and Raleigh were awarded straight A's, while
San Diego received the nation's only A–.

Metro Area	Points	Population Change, 1980–1990
1. Las Vegas	(100)	60.1%
2. Orlando	(90)	53.3%
3. West Palm Beach	(85)	49.7%
4. Austin	(79)	45.6%
5. Phoenix	(71)	40.6%
6. Bakersfield	(63)	34.8%
7. Sacramento	(62)	34.7%
8. San Diego	(62)	34.2%
9. Dallas	(59)	32.6%
10. Atlanta	(59)	32.5%
11. Raleigh	(57)	31.2%
12. Fresno	(55)	29.7%
13. Tampa	(53)	28.2%
14. Los Angeles	(50)	26.4%
15. (tie) Jacksonville	(49)	25.5%
Tucson	(49)	25.5%
17. El Paso	(45)	23.3%
18. Seattle	(44)	22.3%
19. San Antonio	(43)	21.5%
20. Miami	(42)	20.8%
21. Washington	(42)	20.7%
22. Norfolk	(41)	20.3%
23. Houston	(40)	19.7%
24. Charlotte	(40)	19.6%
25. (tie) Charleston	(37)	17.8%
Salt Lake City	(37)	17.8%
27. San Francisco	(35)	16.5%
28. Nashville	(34)	15.8%
29. Minneapolis	(34)	15.3%
30. Grand Rapids	(32)	14.4%
31. Denver	(32)	14.2%

Metro Area	Points	Population Change, 1980–1990
32. Portland	(32)	13.9%
33. Richmond	(31)	13.7%
34. Greenville	(29)	12.4%
35. Oklahoma City	(28)	11.4%
36. Columbus	(27)	10.7%
37. Greensboro	(27)	10.6%
38. Honolulu	(25)	9.7%
39. Kansas City	(25)	9.3%
40. Baltimore	(23)	8.3%
41. (tie) Allentown	(23)	8.1%
Little Rock	(23)	8.1%
43. Tulsa	(23)	7.9%
44. Memphis	(22)	7.5%
45. Indianapolis	(21)	7.1%
46. (tie) Baton Rouge	(21)	6.9%
Hartford	(21)	6.9%
Knoxville	(21)	6.9%
49. Providence	(20)	5.8%
50. (tie) Harrisburg	(19)	5.7%
Omaha	(19)	5.7%
52. New Haven	(19)	5.6%
53. Cincinnati	(19)	5.1%
54. Albany	(18)	4.6%
55. Philadelphia	(17)	3.9%
56. Springfield	(16)	3.6%
57. Boston	(16)	3.3%
58. Rochester	(16)	3.2%
59. New York City	(16)	3.1%
60. Saint Louis	(15)	2.8%
61. Birmingham	(15)	2.7%
62. Syracuse	(15)	2.6%

Metro Area	Points	Population Change, 1980–1990
63. Milwaukee	(15)	2.4%
64. Chicago	(13)	1.6%
65. Dayton	(12)	1.0%
66. Scranton	(12)	0.7%
67. (tie) Louisville	(10)	–0.4%
Toledo	(10)	–0.4%
69. New Orleans	(9)	–1.4%
70. Detroit	(8)	–1.8%
71. Cleveland	(7)	–2.6%
72. Buffalo	(5)	–4.3%
73. Pittsburgh	(0)	–7.4%

Metro Area	Points	Per Capita Income Change, 1984–1989
1. (tie) Baltimore	(100)	49.4%
New York City	(100)	49.4%
3. Boston	(99)	49.0%
4. Hartford	(98)	48.8%
5. Springfield	(97)	48.5%
6. New Haven	(96)	48.1%
7. Las Vegas	(87)	45.4%
8. Philadelphia	(84)	44.4%
9. Albany	(83)	44.0%
10. (tie) Raleigh	(81)	43.5%
Scranton	(81)	43.5%
12. (tie) Grand Rapids	(81)	43.4%
West Palm Beach	(81)	43.4%
14. Richmond	(80)	43.2%
15. Rochester	(80)	43.1%
16. Sacramento	(79)	42.6%
17. Memphis	(78)	42.4%
18. Knoxville	(77)	42.2%
19. Detroit	(76)	41.8%
20. Seattle	(75)	41.4%
21. Nashville	(74)	41.3%
22. Greensboro	(74)	41.0%
23. Washington	(71)	40.2%
24. Greenville	(71)	40.1%
25. Syracuse	(70)	40.0%
26. (tie) Charlotte	(70)	39.8%
Honolulu	(70)	39.8%
28. (tie) Fresno	(69)	39.7%
Orlando	(69)	39.7%
Providence	(69)	39.7%

Metro Area	Points	Per Capita Income Change, 1984–1989
31. Tampa	(69)	39.6%
32. Pittsburgh	(68)	39.4%
33. (tie) Allentown	(68)	39.3%
Buffalo	(68)	39.3%
35. (tie) Chicago	(68)	39.1%
Indianapolis	(68)	39.1%
37. San Francisco	(66)	38.5%
38. San Diego	(65)	38.4%
39. Birmingham	(65)	38.3%
40. Atlanta	(63)	37.6%
41. Los Angeles	(61)	37.1%
42. Portland	(59)	36.5%
43. (tie) Columbus	(58)	36.2%
Louisville	(58)	36.2%
Miami	(58)	36.2%
46. Cincinnati	(57)	35.8%
47. Saint Louis	(56)	35.5%
48. Cleveland	(54)	34.8%
49. Phoenix	(52)	34.1%
50. Dayton	(51)	34.0%
51. Toledo	(51)	33.8%
52. Jacksonville	(49)	33.3%
53. Minneapolis	(49)	33.2%
54. Milwaukee	(47)	32.7%
55. Little Rock	(47)	32.6%
56. Harrisburg	(45)	32.1%
57. Tucson	(41)	30.8%
58. Salt Lake City	(41)	30.6%
59. Bakersfield	(40)	30.5%
60. Kansas City	(37)	29.5%

Metro Area	Points	Per Capita Income Change, 1984–1989
61. Norfolk	(36)	29.1%
62. Omaha	(30)	27.3%
63. Baton Rouge	(21)	24.5%
64. Tulsa	(19)	23.6%
65. Denver	(17)	23.0%
66. El Paso	(16)	22.8%
67. (tie) Dallas	(15)	22.6%
San Antonio	(15)	22.6%
69. Charleston	(15)	22.3%
70. Houston	(14)	22.0%
71. Austin	(6)	19.5%
72. New Orleans	(4)	19.0%
73. Oklahoma City	(0)	17.7%

Metro Area	Points
A+	
1. Las Vegas	94
A	
2. West Palm Beach	83
3. Orlando	80
4. Sacramento	71
5. Raleigh	69
A–	
6. San Diego	64
B+	
7. (tie) Baltimore	62
Fresno	62
Phoenix	62
B	
10. (tie) Atlanta	61
Tampa	61
12. (tie) Hartford	60
Seattle	60
14. (tie) Boston	58
New Haven	58
New York City	58
17. (tie) Grand Rapids	57
Springfield	57
Washington	57
B–	
20. (tie) Los Angeles	56
Richmond	56
22. Charlotte	55
23. Nashville	54

Metro Area	Points
C+	
24. Bakersfield	52
25. (tie) Albany	51
Greensboro	51
Philadelphia	51
San Francisco	51
C	
29. (tie) Greenville	50
Memphis	50
Miami	50
32. (tie) Jacksonville	49
Knoxville	49
34. (tie) Honolulu	48
Rochester	48
36. Scranton	47
37. (tie) Allentown	46
Portland	46
39. (tie) Indianapolis	45
Providence	45
Tucson	45
42. (tie) Austin	43
Columbus	43
Syracuse	43
45. (tie) Detroit	42
Minneapolis	42
47. Chicago	41
48. Birmingham	40
49. (tie) Norfolk	39
Salt Lake City	39
51. Cincinnati	38

Metro Area	Points
C–	
52. (tie) Buffalo	37
Dallas	37
54. Saint Louis	36
55. Little Rock	35
56. (tie) Louisville	34
Pittsburgh	34
D+	
58. (tie) Dayton	32
Harrisburg	32
D	
60. (tie) Cleveland	31
El Paso	31
Kansas City	31
Milwaukee	31
Toledo	31
65. San Antonio	29
66. Houston	27
67. Charleston	26
D–	
68. (tie) Denver	25
Omaha	25
F	
70. (tie) Baton Rouge	21
Tulsa	21
72. Oklahoma City	14
73. New Orleans	7

Test No. 2: Future Growth   33

Much has been written in the past two decades about the exodus of Easterners and Midwesterners to the warmer climes of the South and West.
It usually is treated as a relatively new phenomenon, though Nestor Terleckyj
says it really isn't.

"It is as old as the country," says Terleckyj, president of NPA Data
Services, a Washington demographics firm. "People have been moving west
since the beginning of the republic—and south since World War II and
the invention of air conditioning. It may be slowing down somewhat, but
I certainly don't see it coming to a halt."

Neither does the U.S. Bureau of Economic Analysis, which is the government agency assigned the duty of foreseeing population trends. The bureau
predicts that of the 20 major metro areas that will grow most quickly in
the future, eleven will be in the West and eight in the South. Washington
will be the only representative from the East; the Midwest will be shut out.

The bureau's 30-year population projections make up the first component of the future growth test. At the top of the list is the West Palm
Beach area, which is expected to increase from a 1990 total of 863,500 residents
to a 2020 figure of 1.26 million. That would be a jump of 45.6 percent.

West Palm Beach's growth will be fueled by two groups of immigrants:

1. Young workers are attracted by the area's high-technology industries
and flourishing service sector, which will remain powerful magnets well
into the next century. The Bureau of Economic Analysis estimates that
West Palm Beach will add 220,000 jobs during the 30-year period, including
114,000 new service jobs.

2. Older people began moving to the area in greater numbers in the
1980s, says Carol Taylor West, an economic forecaster at the University
of Florida. She predicts that the influx of retirees will slow in the 1990s,
but will accelerate early in the 21st century as the first baby boomers reach
Social Security age.

"Way back, retirees went to Saint Petersburg. Then it was Sarasota,"
says West. "Then they started trying the east coast, like Palm Beach County.
It's word of mouth. You see it start slowly in a place like Palm Beach,
and then it picks up."

Warm weather is the common denominator in areas that are expected
to experience the strongest population growth in the future. West Palm
Beach is joined in the national top five by Phoenix, Las Vegas, San Diego,
and Tampa. Each of these metros is projected to expand more than 36
percent by 2020.

"Weather is something that will always work in their favor," says Paul
Getman, managing director of Regional Financial Associates, an economic

34 forecasting firm. "Older people leave the Northeast and Midwest in droves because of the climate, and there is nothing that can be done about that."

But these growth centers have more than nice temperatures going for them. Unique local factors also can trigger future population expansion, which is expected to be the case in two California metros.

San Diego, No. 4 nationally in projected population growth, will benefit greatly from its location on the Pacific Ocean and the Mexican border, says Stephen Levy, director of the Center for Continuing Study of the California Economy. He says San Diego is poised to become an important international trade center, particularly if the United States and Mexico implement a free trade agreement.

Location also is the key—but in a completely different way—for Sacramento, which ranks eighth in projected population growth.

"Sacramento could really be called low-cost competition," says Levy. "Of the major metro areas in the state, it has the lowest land prices, which translates into the lowest living costs. And it has proximity [to San Francisco] going for it, so it benefits from the spillover effect."

The other end of the projected population growth spectrum is a two-state affair. Four of the bottom six metros are in upstate New York: Buffalo, Rochester, Albany, and Syracuse. The other two are in Louisiana: New Orleans and bottom-ranked Baton Rouge, where the population is expected to increase only 1.5 percent by 2020.

"The 1980s were a tough period for Louisiana in general," says Karen Paterson, the Louisiana state demographer. "After oil prices dropped in 1983, things went sour. But they've been picking up since 1987, which is why I'm skeptical about some of these projections. They're based on our worst period. If you base [the future] on our low point, the figures will be lower than they should be."

The second component of this test is rooted firmly in the present. It is based on the simple theory that future growth requires open space. The lower the population density, the higher a metro area's score.

Nowhere will you find more room to grow than in Bakersfield, which has 543,000 residents spread out over 8,141 square miles. That works out to only 67 persons per square mile, the lowest density to be found in any major metropolitan area.

Two other areas join Bakersfield in having fewer than 100 persons per square mile: Tucson and Las Vegas. Mountains and deserts are responsible for the low densities in these metros, but the arid terrain also places a burden on future development.

"Sure, Las Vegas has potential problems with water, just because it is not easily obtained," says Jeff Hardcastle, a planning official with Clark County, Nevada. "Without additional sources, things could cap out fairly early in the next century. But that's not likely to happen. The [Las Vegas] water district is already pursuing alternatives."

It comes as no surprise that New York City is the most crowded metro area in the country, with a population density of 2,354 persons per square mile. Nor is it a shock that Boston and Chicago are next on the list.

What *is* surprising is that the New York City metro encompasses only 7,627 square miles, 514 fewer than Bakersfield. That means the New York City area would have just 511,000 residents if its density were the same as Bakersfield's.

The A+ metro area for future growth. Las Vegas ranked No. 1 on this test, the result of impressive third-place finishes in both components. The Bureau of Economic Analysis predicts that the population of the Las Vegas area will expand from 741,000 in 1990 to 1.04 million in 2020, a jump of 39.9 percent. Many of these newcomers to Las Vegas are expected to arrive from Los Angeles.

"There's really not a good way to track that, but I've seen some estimates that 40 percent of our new residents are from southern California," says Hardcastle. "It's a good trade for them. They can sell their property there and buy much larger housing here at a lower price."

Arizona, California, and Florida equally divided the other six slots in the A range on this test. Phoenix, West Palm Beach, Tucson, and Sacramento received straight A's. Grades of A– were awarded to Bakersfield and Jacksonville.

Metro Area	Points	Projected Population Change, 1990–2020
1. West Palm Beach	(100)	45.6%
2. Phoenix	(92)	42.0%
3. Las Vegas	(87)	39.9%
4. San Diego	(81)	37.1%
5. Tampa	(79)	36.5%
6. Orlando	(76)	35.0%
7. Jacksonville	(75)	34.8%
8. Sacramento	(75)	34.6%
9. Denver	(70)	32.4%
10. Honolulu	(69)	31.8%
11. Tucson	(68)	31.7%
12. Atlanta	(61)	28.5%
13. Salt Lake City	(61)	28.3%
14. Los Angeles	(59)	27.4%
15. Bakersfield	(57)	26.6%
16. Norfolk	(56)	26.1%
17. Washington	(56)	26.0%
18. Richmond	(53)	25.0%
19. Seattle	(52)	24.6%
20. Memphis	(51)	23.9%
21. Nashville	(49)	23.2%
22. Portland	(48)	22.6%
23. Omaha	(47)	22.1%
24. (tie) Knoxville	(46)	21.9%
San Francisco	(46)	21.9%
26. Minneapolis	(45)	21.2%
27. Kansas City	(44)	20.9%
28. San Antonio	(43)	20.7%
29. Indianapolis	(42)	20.0%
30. Fresno	(41)	19.7%

Metro Area	Points	Projected Population Change, 1990–2020
31. Philadelphia	(40)	19.3%
32. Miami	(40)	19.1%
33. Charleston	(39)	18.8%
34. Tulsa	(39)	18.6%
35. Baltimore	(38)	18.0%
36. Providence	(37)	17.7%
37. (tie) Chicago	(37)	17.6%
El Paso	(37)	17.6%
39. Grand Rapids	(36)	17.5%
40. New Haven	(36)	17.3%
41. Austin	(35)	16.9%
42. Hartford	(35)	16.8%
43. Dallas	(34)	16.6%
44. Raleigh	(34)	16.5%
45. Allentown	(34)	16.4%
46. Harrisburg	(32)	15.6%
47. Greensboro	(32)	15.5%
48. Charlotte	(32)	15.4%
49. Boston	(31)	15.3%
50. Little Rock	(31)	15.2%
51. Houston	(30)	14.8%
52. Oklahoma City	(30)	14.7%
53. Columbus	(30)	14.6%
54. Saint Louis	(29)	14.2%
55. (tie) Louisville	(28)	13.8%
Springfield	(28)	13.8%
57. Scranton	(27)	13.2%
58. New York City	(26)	13.0%
59. Birmingham	(26)	12.9%
60. Cincinnati	(24)	12.0%

Metro Area	Points	Projected Population Change, 1990–2020
61. Pittsburgh	(22)	11.2%
62. Greenville	(21)	10.9%
63. Milwaukee	(21)	10.6%
64. Dayton	(20)	10.2%
65. Toledo	(19)	9.9%
66. Detroit	(19)	9.7%
67. Cleveland	(17)	9.2%
68. Syracuse	(15)	8.1%
69. New Orleans	(14)	7.6%
70. Albany	(13)	7.3%
71. Rochester	(9)	5.6%
72. Buffalo	(8)	4.9%
73. Baton Rouge	(0)	1.5%

Metro Area	Points	Persons Per Square Mile
1. Bakersfield	(100)	67
2. Tucson	(100)	73
3. Las Vegas	(98)	94
4. Fresno	(97)	112
5. Tulsa	(95)	141
6. Little Rock	(93)	176
7. Charleston	(91)	196
8. Knoxville	(90)	218
9. Oklahoma City	(89)	226
10. Birmingham	(89)	228
11. Phoenix	(89)	231
12. Nashville	(88)	242
13. Scranton	(87)	259
14. Albany	(86)	269
15. Greensboro	(86)	273
16. Syracuse	(86)	276
17. Austin	(86)	280
18. Sacramento	(85)	291
19. Richmond	(85)	294
20. Harrisburg	(85)	295
21. Greenville	(84)	305
22. Kansas City	(83)	314
23. Omaha	(83)	323
24. Baton Rouge	(82)	333
25. Portland	(82)	338
26. Rochester	(81)	342
27. (tie) Charlotte	(81)	344
Jacksonville	(81)	344
29. Raleigh	(80)	365
30. Columbus	(79)	385
31. Indianapolis	(77)	407

Metro Area	Points	Persons Per Square Mile
32. Denver	(77)	410
33. Louisville	(76)	420
34. Orlando	(76)	423
35. West Palm Beach	(76)	424
36. Memphis	(76)	426
37. Los Angeles	(76)	428
38. Seattle	(75)	434
39. Toledo	(74)	450
40. Saint Louis	(74)	458
41. Allentown	(73)	470
42. Grand Rapids	(72)	484
43. Minneapolis	(72)	488
44. San Antonio	(70)	517
45. Houston	(69)	522
46. Springfield	(69)	525
47. New Orleans	(68)	537
48. Atlanta	(67)	553
49. Dallas	(67)	558
50. Dayton	(66)	565
51. El Paso	(65)	584
52. Pittsburgh	(65)	585
53. San Diego	(64)	594
54. Salt Lake City	(60)	663
55. Cincinnati	(59)	673
56. Hartford	(55)	742
57. Buffalo	(53)	759
58. Tampa	(50)	810
59. Norfolk	(49)	828
60. San Francisco	(47)	849
61. Milwaukee	(44)	896
62. Detroit	(44)	901

Metro Area	Points	Persons Per Square Mile
63. Baltimore	(43)	913
64. Cleveland	(41)	948
65. Providence	(39)	974
66. Washington	(38)	989
67. Miami	(36)	1,012
68. Philadelphia	(30)	1,104
69. New Haven	(15)	1,328
70. Honolulu	(11)	1,393
71. Chicago	(8)	1,435
72. Boston	(0)	1,551
73. New York City	(0)	2,354

Future Growth: Scores and Grades

Metro Area	Points
A+	
1. Las Vegas	93
A	
2. Phoenix	91
3. West Palm Beach	88
4. Tucson	84
5. Sacramento	80
A–	
6. Bakersfield	79
7. Jacksonville	78
B+	
8. Orlando	76
9. Denver	74
10. San Diego	73
B	
11. (tie) Fresno	69
Nashville	69
Richmond	69
14. (tie) Knoxville	68
Los Angeles	68
16. Tulsa	67
17. (tie) Charleston	65
Omaha	65
Portland	65
Tampa	65
B–	
21. (tie) Atlanta	64
Kansas City	64
Memphis	64
Seattle	64
25. Little Rock	62

Metro Area	Points

<table>
<tr><td colspan="2" align="center">C+</td></tr>
</table>

Metro Area	Points
26. (tie) Austin	61
Salt Lake City	61
28. (tie) Indianapolis	60
Oklahoma City	60
30. (tie) Greensboro	59
Harrisburg	59
Minneapolis	59

<table>
<tr><td colspan="2" align="center">C</td></tr>
</table>

Metro Area	Points
33. Birmingham	58
34. (tie) Charlotte	57
Raleigh	57
San Antonio	57
Scranton	57
38. Columbus	55
39. (tie) Allentown	54
Grand Rapids	54
41. (tie) Greenville	53
Norfolk	53
43. (tie) Louisville	52
Saint Louis	52
45. (tie) Dallas	51
El Paso	51
Syracuse	51
48. (tie) Albany	50
Houston	50
50. Springfield	49

Metro Area	Points
C–	
51. (tie) San Francisco	47
Toledo	47
Washington	47
54. (tie) Hartford	45
Rochester	45
56. Pittsburgh	44
57. Dayton	43
58. Cincinnati	42
D+	
59. (tie) Baltimore	41
Baton Rouge	41
New Orleans	41
D	
62. Honolulu	40
63. (tie) Miami	38
Providence	38
65. Philadelphia	35
66. Milwaukee	33
67. Detroit	32
D–	
68. Buffalo	31
69. Cleveland	29
F	
70. New Haven	26
71. Chicago	23
72. Boston	16
73. New York City	13

Test No. 3: Job Opportunities   **45**

It's a chicken and egg kind of question. Which comes first: population growth or job growth? Does a wave of new residents spur the creation of jobs, or does the creation of jobs lure the new residents?

Chicken, egg, chicken, egg. We could go back and forth on this point all day. The logical answer is that the two should feed off of each other. The best way to sustain a healthy economy is to combine steady population increases with rapid expansion of the local employment base.

That's exactly the formula being followed by several Southern and Western metros. The 20 areas that had the nation's strongest rates of population growth in the 1980s were all in the South or West. The same can be said for sixteen of the 20 areas that created jobs at the fastest pace.

Job growth during the latter half of the 1980s is the first component of the job opportunities test. At the top of the list is Las Vegas, which added 124,000 jobs between 1985 and 1990, an increase of 48.9 percent. According to Frank MacDonald, state labor commissioner of Nevada, Las Vegas provides a perfect example of the cyclical connection between population growth and employment-base expansion.

"Most of the growth in Las Vegas is because of construction," Mac-Donald says. "The construction of new casinos and resort hotels brings new employment, which brings more people to live here. And then the opening [of the new attractions] brings in more tourists who want to see whatever is new and spectacular. And that inspires more interest in construction."

Five other metros increased their job totals by more than 25 percent during the latter half of the 1980s. All are in the South or West: Orlando, Seattle, Sacramento, San Diego, and West Palm Beach.

Orlando, No. 2 nationally with job growth of 37.8 percent from 1985 to 1990, comes closest to duplicating the Las Vegas pattern of growth fueled by construction and tourism. The ongoing expansion of Walt Disney World and the opening of other massive theme parks resulted in an ever-expanding employment base in the 1980s.

"Most people don't know it, but Disney already employs about 33,000 people and keeps adding on with new products," says David Scott, director of the Orlando-based Phillips Institute for the Study of American Business Activity. "You can see their impact throughout central Florida. In the '80s, we had an extraordinary expansion in the number of hotel rooms, essentially doubling the number to about 78,000 rooms."

The recession of 1990–1992 has tested Orlando's economic balance; the area actually lost 14,100 jobs in 1991. But it had regained all of them by April 1992, resuming its forward movement at a time when much of the country still was in a recession.

46   Lacking such resilience were the areas at the bottom of the job growth list, a predictable mix of metros hit by the energy bust of the 1980s—Denver, New Orleans, and last-place Oklahoma City—and Eastern areas dependent on the ailing financial sector—Boston, Springfield, and New York City.

"The Northeast really suffered the most of the four regions in the recession," says Mary Stewart, a spokeswoman for Manpower Inc., an employment firm based in Milwaukee. "It was crippled in key industries, particularly finance, insurance, and real estate. The Northeast had been riding very, very high in the late '80s, but it had a much more severe drop after that."

The rate at which a metro area's employment base expands is one measure of local job opportunities. Another important indicator is an area's unemployment rate, the subject of this test's second component.

The top score goes to Raleigh for its average unemployment rate of 2.8 percent from 1985 through 1990. (That figure is calculated by averaging the area's annual jobless rates during the six-year period.) Raleigh's rate is roughly half of the national median of 5.4 percent for the same time span.

"That's amazing, isn't it?" remarks Greg Sampson, research director for the North Carolina Employment Security Commission. "There are lots of periods when [Raleigh's jobless rate] falls under 2 percent, which seems almost impossible, and it rarely ranges above 4 percent."

Unemployment remains low in Raleigh because the area is blessed with stable employers, including several large research firms, three major universities, and the North Carolina state government.

The benefits of having a strong government sector are obvious. The five areas with the nation's lowest jobless rates are capitals: Raleigh, Boston, Honolulu, and Hartford on the state level, Washington on the federal. (The low rates in Boston and Hartford largely reflect the East's economic boom in the mid-1980s; unemployment worsened in those two areas in the early 1990s.)

Agriculture is a major component of the Fresno area's economy, meaning that thousands of local jobs are seasonal. Unemployment soars each year from October to March. This instability is one of the reasons that Fresno had the nation's highest average annual jobless rate for 1985–1990, 11.1 percent.

"We've also had a couple of major manufacturers close their doors, and that snowballs a lot of things," says Rosemary Rusca, a supervisor at the Fresno office of the California Employment Development Department. "People make less, so they spend less. So then retail falls off."

Four other metro areas had average annual unemployment rates above 8 percent during the six-year period: El Paso, Bakersfield, New Orleans, and Baton Rouge.

The A+ metro area for job opportunities. Orlando received the highest score on this test, largely because of its second-place finish in the job growth component. The Orlando area's average unemployment rate of 4.8 percent ranked 23rd, but still was comfortably below the national median of 5.4 percent.

"The decade of golden growth in central Florida was the 1980s," says Scott. "We can't match that rate in the 1990s; nobody could. You simply don't have an EPCOT or a Universal Studios Florida opening every decade. But on a national basis, our growth rate for jobs is still going to be very, very good."

It was only natural that the West and South, the centers of future population growth, also dominated the job opportunities test. Las Vegas, Raleigh, Seattle, and San Diego were awarded straight A's, while Charlotte and Honolulu received grades of A–.

Metro Area	Points	Change in Number of Non-Farm Jobs, 1985-1990
1. Las Vegas	(100)	48.9%
2. Orlando	(100)	37.8%
3. Seattle	(82)	30.8%
4. Sacramento	(74)	28.1%
5. San Diego	(72)	27.3%
6. West Palm Beach	(70)	26.4%
7. Portland	(61)	22.9%
8. Raleigh	(59)	22.1%
9. Grand Rapids	(58)	21.9%
10. Charlotte	(58)	21.8%
11. (tie) Fresno	(56)	21.2%
Tampa	(56)	21.2%
13. Indianapolis	(56)	21.1%
14. Charleston	(55)	20.6%
15. Honolulu	(53)	20.1%
16. Columbus	(51)	19.2%
17. Richmond	(50)	18.7%
18. (tie) Cincinnati	(49)	18.4%
Greenville	(49)	18.4%
20. Jacksonville	(49)	18.3%
21. Nashville	(47)	17.8%
22. Los Angeles	(47)	17.6%
23. Washington	(47)	17.5%
24. Phoenix	(46)	17.4%
25. El Paso	(45)	17.0%
26. Louisville	(45)	16.8%
27. Atlanta	(44)	16.6%
28. Knoxville	(42)	15.9%
29. Miami	(42)	15.8%
30. Memphis	(41)	15.2%

Metro Area	Points	Change in Number of Non-Farm Jobs, 1985–1990
31. Norfolk	(40)	15.0%
32. Little Rock	(39)	14.6%
33. Birmingham	(39)	14.5%
34. (tie) Greensboro	(38)	14.4%
Omaha	(38)	14.4%
36. Harrisburg	(38)	14.2%
37. Milwaukee	(38)	14.1%
38. Albany	(37)	13.9%
39. Salt Lake City	(36)	13.6%
40. (tie) Baltimore	(34)	12.9%
Minneapolis	(34)	12.9%
42. Kansas City	(33)	12.2%
43. Scranton	(32)	12.0%
44. Bakersfield	(32)	11.8%
45. Detroit	(31)	11.6%
46. Saint Louis	(30)	11.3%
47. (tie) Buffalo	(30)	11.1%
San Francisco	(30)	11.1%
49. Dayton	(29)	10.9%
50. Chicago	(28)	10.4%
51. Syracuse	(27)	10.1%
52. Toledo	(27)	9.9%
53. (tie) Allentown	(26)	9.6%
Cleveland	(26)	9.6%
55. Philadelphia	(26)	9.5%
56. (tie) Baton Rouge	(25)	9.3%
New Haven	(25)	9.3%
Tucson	(25)	9.3%
59. Rochester	(23)	8.6%
60. San Antonio	(22)	8.2%

Metro Area	Points	Change in Number of Non-Farm Jobs, 1985–1990
61. Dallas	(22)	8.0%
62. Hartford	(21)	7.8%
63. Pittsburgh	(20)	7.5%
64. Houston	(20)	7.3%
65. Providence	(17)	6.4%
66. Austin	(14)	5.2%
67. Tulsa	(14)	5.0%
68. New York City	(12)	4.2%
69. Springfield	(11)	4.1%
70. Denver	(10)	3.5%
71. Boston	(5)	1.7%
72. New Orleans	(1)	0.1%
73. Oklahoma City	(0)	–0.2%

Metro Area	Points	Average Annual Unemployment Rate, 1985–1990
1. Raleigh	(100)	2.8%
2. Washington	(95)	3.2%
3. (tie) Boston	(92)	3.5%
Honolulu	(92)	3.5%
5. Hartford	(90)	3.6%
6. Greensboro	(88)	3.8%
7. (tie) Charlotte	(87)	3.9%
New Haven	(87)	3.9%
9. Richmond	(86)	4.0%
10. Minneapolis	(84)	4.1%
11. (tie) Charleston	(83)	4.2%
Springfield	(83)	4.2%
13. (tie) Albany	(82)	4.3%
Providence	(82)	4.3%
15. (tie) Greenville	(81)	4.4%
Harrisburg	(81)	4.4%
Nashville	(81)	4.4%
Omaha	(81)	4.4%
19. Rochester	(80)	4.5%
20. San Diego	(78)	4.6%
21. (tie) Philadelphia	(77)	4.7%
San Francisco	(77)	4.7%
23. (tie) Norfolk	(76)	4.8%
Orlando	(76)	4.8%
25. (tie) Atlanta	(75)	4.9%
Baltimore	(75)	4.9%
Indianapolis	(75)	4.9%
Phoenix	(75)	4.9%
Salt Lake City	(75)	4.9%
Tampa	(75)	4.9%

Metro Area	Points	Average Annual Unemployment Rate, 1985–1990
31. (tie) Kansas City	(73)	5.0%
Milwaukee	(73)	5.0%
Tucson	(73)	5.0%
34. New York City	(72)	5.1%
35. Seattle	(70)	5.3%
36. (tie) Austin	(69)	5.4%
Columbus	(69)	5.4%
Jacksonville	(69)	5.4%
Los Angeles	(69)	5.4%
40. Syracuse	(67)	5.5%
41. (tie) Cincinnati	(66)	5.6%
Memphis	(66)	5.6%
Portland	(66)	5.6%
44. (tie) Dallas	(65)	5.7%
Denver	(65)	5.7%
Oklahoma City	(65)	5.7%
Sacramento	(65)	5.7%
48. (tie) Allentown	(64)	5.8%
Dayton	(64)	5.8%
Miami	(64)	5.8%
West Palm Beach	(64)	5.8%
52. Buffalo	(63)	5.9%
53. Las Vegas	(60)	6.1%
54. (tie) Cleveland	(58)	6.3%
Knoxville	(58)	6.3%
56. Saint Louis	(57)	6.4%
57. (tie) Grand Rapids	(55)	6.5%
Little Rock	(55)	6.5%
Louisville	(55)	6.5%
60. Birmingham	(54)	6.6%

Metro Area	Points	Average Annual Unemployment Rate, 1985–1990
61. Chicago	(53)	6.7%
62. Pittsburgh	(52)	6.8%
63. (tie) Toledo	(48)	7.1%
Tulsa	(48)	7.1%
65. (tie) San Antonio	(47)	7.2%
Scranton	(47)	7.2%
67. Houston	(42)	7.6%
68. Detroit	(41)	7.7%
69. Baton Rouge	(28)	8.8%
70. New Orleans	(25)	9.0%
71. (tie) Bakersfield	(4)	10.8%
El Paso	(4)	10.8%
73. Fresno	(0)	11.1%

Metro Area	Points
A+	
1. Orlando	88
A	
2. (tie) Las Vegas	80
Raleigh	80
4. Seattle	76
5. San Diego	75
A–	
6. (tie) Charlotte	73
Honolulu	73
B+	
8. Washington	71
9. Sacramento	70
B	
10. Charleston	69
11. Richmond	68
12. West Palm Beach	67
13. (tie) Indianapolis	66
Tampa	66
15. Greenville	65
16. (tie) Nashville	64
Portland	64
18. Greensboro	63
19. Phoenix	61
B–	
20. (tie) Albany	60
Atlanta	60
Columbus	60
Harrisburg	60
Omaha	60

Metro Area	Points
25. (tie) Jacksonville	59
Minneapolis	59

C+

Metro Area	Points
27. (tie) Cincinnati	58
Los Angeles	58
Norfolk	58
30. Grand Rapids	57
31. (tie) Hartford	56
Milwaukee	56
New Haven	56
Salt Lake City	56

C

Metro Area	Points
35. Baltimore	55
36. (tie) Memphis	54
San Francisco	54
38. (tie) Kansas City	53
Miami	53
40. (tie) Philadelphia	52
Rochester	52
42. (tie) Knoxville	50
Louisville	50
Providence	50
45. (tie) Boston	49
Tucson	49
47. (tie) Birmingham	47
Buffalo	47
Dayton	47
Little Rock	47
Springfield	47
Syracuse	47

Metro Area	Points
53. Allentown	45
54. (tie) Dallas	44
Saint Louis	44

C–

56. (tie) Austin	42
Cleveland	42
New York City	42
59. Chicago	41
60. Scranton	40

D+

61. (tie) Denver	38
Toledo	38

D

63. (tie) Detroit	36
Pittsburgh	36
65. San Antonio	35
66. Oklahoma City	33

D–

67. (tie) Houston	31
Tulsa	31

F

69. Fresno	28
70. Baton Rouge	27
71. El Paso	25
72. Bakersfield	18
73. New Orleans	13

Test No. 4: Business Opportunities

Where is the best place to start your own business? The answer seems immediately obvious. Find an area where there won't be much competition. Strive to be the only game in town, if you can.

Wrong, says Alan Weinstein, director of the Buffalo-based Canisius College Center for Entrepreneurship. The ideal location for a new business is a place that already has plenty of new businesses.

"Entrepreneurship tends to breed entrepreneurship," says Weinstein. "It's a matter of community support. If there are a lot of role models around, that's a big help. People learn from other people."

But wait a minute. People also *compete* with other people. Isn't a crowded market an automatic guarantee that a new business will have difficulty lining up financing and attracting customers?

"To me it says the opposite," says Weinstein. "It tells me that this is a growth area, that there is some capital around, that the community is very supportive, that there are people around with good strong technical backgrounds. When there are a lot of entrepreneurial ventures, there are lots of opportunities for people."

Most of those opportunities are found in the retail and service sectors, which together include 60 percent of all companies in the United States. The two sectors are attractive to budding entrepreneurs for a simple reason: The cost of starting a small store or service firm is only a fraction of what it takes to set up a manufacturing operation or construction company.

The first component of the business opportunities test measures the health of each area's retail sector by comparing the total number of stores with the local population. West Palm Beach is in first place with a ratio of 727 retail establishments per 100,000 residents.

"A number of things help push up retail sales around here," says Michael Geiger, research director for the Palm Beach County Business Development Board. "We've got strong tourism, which means there are always new customers. We're one of the fastest-growing areas in the country. And to be honest, there are pockets of affluence here; there is a certain amount of money."

Geiger is guilty of understatement. A case can be made that residents of the West Palm Beach area have more spending money than people in any other metropolitan area. Washington is the only metro that surpasses West Palm Beach in per capita income, but the tables are turned when it comes to disposable income. The cost of living in the nation's capital region is much steeper. The typical house in Washington, for example, costs about 75 percent more than the average house in West Palm Beach.

Strong retail sectors are concentrated in the South and the East. Six

58 areas besides West Palm Beach have ratios of more than 650 stores per 100,000 residents: Knoxville, Miami, Greensboro, Scranton, Raleigh, and Providence.

It should be no surprise that areas with low income levels dominate the bottom of the retail list. El Paso and Salt Lake City are tied for last place, each with only 483 retail establishments per 100,000. El Paso has the lowest per capita income of all 73 major metros, while Salt Lake City is only two positions higher.

"We have the entrepreneurial drive here in El Paso. But we need the resources, and we don't have them," says Henry King, director of the Small Business Institute at the University of Texas-El Paso. "Our financial resources are low, and our human resources unfortunately are not what they should be. The median education level here is slightly less than the 12th grade."

The story is different in Denver, where hardy entrepreneurial spirit and ample economic resources have combined to form a vibrant service sector. The Denver area has 19,884 service businesses, ranging from advertising agencies to auto repair shops and dance studios to dental clinics. That works out to a ratio of 1,076 service establishments per 100,000 residents, earning Denver the highest score in this test's second component.

"We have so many small businesses here because we have a collection of people who are willing to take risks," says Richard Wobbekind, director of the Business Research Division of the University of Colorado.

"People here do adventurous things in their spare time," he says. "They ski, they hang glide, they bungee jump—all the things that other people consider insane. And a lot of the people here are not natives of Denver. I think people who set out on their own are also risk-takers."

Denver easily outdistances the rest of the heartland in this component. It is, in fact, the only area from the nation's interior to finish in the top 10 percent of the service sector list. The other leaders are spread out along the Atlantic (West Palm Beach, Miami, Washington, and Boston) or the Pacific (San Francisco and Seattle).

Last place again belongs to El Paso, which has only 565 service establishments per 100,000 residents.

"We have the spirit here," says King. "But when the kids get the skills, they take them elsewhere so they can make more money. I don't blame them; I encourage them. Hopefully, some of them will return after they have established themselves."

Joining El Paso at the bottom of the service sector list are two metros from the South, Charleston and Norfolk, and two from the West, Bakersfield and Fresno.

The A+ metro area for business opportunities. West Palm Beach took first place on this test because of its outstanding performances in both components. It ranked first in retail sector strength and second in service sector strength.

"This is an outstanding location with a lot of strong entrepreneurial spirit," says Thomas Pledger, chief executive officer of Dycom Industries, a West Palm Beach telecommunications engineering firm. "I moved here in 1963 when it was sort of a sleepy resort that only bustled in the winter. But now we're a real metro area with cultural events and colleges and clean, technical industry. We have grown up."

Straight A's on this test went to Miami, Knoxville, Denver, and Raleigh. Grades of A– were awarded to Boston and San Francisco.

Metro Area	Points	Retail Establishments Per 100,000 Residents
1. West Palm Beach	(100)	727
2. Knoxville	(93)	711
3. Miami	(83)	686
4. (tie) Greensboro	(72)	658
Scranton	(72)	658
6. Raleigh	(71)	657
7. Providence	(70)	655
8. New Haven	(64)	639
9. (tie) Jacksonville	(64)	638
Springfield	(64)	638
11. Hartford	(63)	636
12. Albany	(61)	633
13. Little Rock	(60)	630
14. Greenville	(60)	629
15. Charlotte	(59)	628
16. Orlando	(59)	627
17. (tie) Buffalo	(58)	624
Nashville	(58)	624
19. (tie) Boston	(56)	620
Omaha	(56)	620
21. (tie) Harrisburg	(56)	619
New York City	(56)	619
Oklahoma City	(56)	619
24. Syracuse	(55)	616
25. (tie) Atlanta	(54)	614
Tampa	(54)	614
27. Tulsa	(53)	613
28. Denver	(52)	611
29. Toledo	(51)	607
30. Pittsburgh	(50)	604

Metro Area	Points	Retail Establishments Per 100,000 Residents
31. San Francisco	(49)	603
32. Kansas City	(48)	601
33. (tie) Allentown	(48)	599
Indianapolis	(48)	599
35. Richmond	(45)	594
36. Charleston	(45)	593
37. Honolulu	(45)	592
38. (tie) Portland	(44)	591
Saint Louis	(44)	591
40. Louisville	(44)	590
41. Seattle	(43)	589
42. Birmingham	(43)	588
43. Cleveland	(41)	583
44. Milwaukee	(41)	582
45. Austin	(38)	576
46. Dallas	(38)	575
47. (tie) Baltimore	(37)	574
Philadelphia	(37)	574
49. (tie) Norfolk	(36)	570
Tucson	(36)	570
51. Memphis	(35)	569
52. New Orleans	(32)	562
53. Columbus	(32)	561
54. Cincinnati	(32)	560
55. Grand Rapids	(30)	556
56. Minneapolis	(30)	555
57. Washington	(27)	550
58. Rochester	(27)	549
59. Dayton	(26)	546

Metro Area	Points	Retail Establishments Per 100,000 Residents
60. (tie) Sacramento	(23)	540
San Antonio	(23)	540
62. Phoenix	(23)	538
63. Detroit	(21)	534
64. Chicago	(20)	531
65. San Diego	(17)	525
66. (tie) Baton Rouge	(14)	517
Fresno	(14)	517
68. Las Vegas	(13)	514
69. Houston	(11)	511
70. Bakersfield	(6)	498
71. Los Angeles	(5)	494
72. (tie) El Paso	(0)	483
Salt Lake City	(0)	483

Metro Area	Points	Service Establishments Per 100,000 Residents
1. Denver	(100)	1,076
2. West Palm Beach	(95)	1,052
3. Miami	(95)	1,049
4. Washington	(92)	1,034
5. San Francisco	(83)	989
6. Boston	(77)	961
7. Seattle	(71)	928
8. Nashville	(70)	922
9. Portland	(69)	919
10. Raleigh	(69)	918
11. (tie) Little Rock	(69)	917
New York City	(69)	917
13. Austin	(68)	911
14. Orlando	(68)	910
15. Atlanta	(67)	908
16. (tie) Hartford	(64)	894
Knoxville	(64)	894
18. New Haven	(64)	891
19. Tampa	(62)	884
20. Phoenix	(61)	875
21. Tulsa	(60)	873
22. Providence	(60)	872
23. Minneapolis	(59)	867
24. Oklahoma City	(59)	866
25. Kansas City	(59)	865
26. Dallas	(57)	855
27. Richmond	(56)	850
28. Los Angeles	(55)	845
29. Omaha	(54)	843
30. Jacksonville	(54)	841

Metro Area	Points	Service Establishments Per 100,000 Residents
31. Indianapolis	(53)	837
32. Philadelphia	(51)	828
33. Saint Louis	(51)	826
34. Tucson	(51)	824
35. Milwaukee	(50)	819
36. Harrisburg	(49)	816
37. New Orleans	(49)	813
38. Charlotte	(48)	812
39. Pittsburgh	(48)	810
40. (tie) Honolulu	(47)	806
San Diego	(47)	806
42. Louisville	(47)	803
43. (tie) Baton Rouge	(45)	797
Cleveland	(45)	797
Toledo	(45)	797
46. Sacramento	(45)	796
47. (tie) Allentown	(44)	792
Columbus	(44)	792
49. Chicago	(43)	786
50. Grand Rapids	(43)	785
51. Albany	(43)	784
52. (tie) Baltimore	(42)	779
Houston	(42)	779
54. Greensboro	(41)	775
55. Detroit	(40)	768
56. Birmingham	(38)	761
57. Greenville	(38)	760
58. Cincinnati	(37)	755
59. Springfield	(36)	750
60. Dayton	(34)	741

Metro Area	Points	Service Establishments Per 100,000 Residents
61. Salt Lake City	(34)	740
62. San Antonio	(34)	737
63. (tie) Buffalo	(33)	733
Memphis	(33)	733
65. Syracuse	(32)	730
66. (tie) Las Vegas	(31)	722
Scranton	(31)	722
68. Rochester	(29)	715
69. Fresno	(28)	706
70. Norfolk	(26)	699
71. Charleston	(25)	694
72. Bakersfield	(7)	599
73. El Paso	(0)	565

Metro Area	Points
A+	
1. West Palm Beach	98
A	
2. Miami	89
3. Knoxville	79
4. Denver	76
5. Raleigh	70
A−	
6. Boston	67
7. San Francisco	66
B+	
8. (tie) Little Rock	65
Providence	65
10. (tie) Hartford	64
Nashville	64
New Haven	64
Orlando	64
B	
14. New York City	63
15. Atlanta	61
16. Washington	60
17. Jacksonville	59
18. (tie) Oklahoma City	58
Tampa	58
20. (tie) Greensboro	57
Portland	57
Seattle	57
Tulsa	57

Metro Area	Points
B–	
24. Omaha	55
25. (tie) Charlotte	54
Kansas City	54
C+	
27. (tie) Austin	53
Harrisburg	53
29. (tie) Albany	52
Scranton	52
31. (tie) Indianapolis	51
Richmond	51
C	
33. Springfield	50
34. (tie) Greenville	49
Pittsburgh	49
36. (tie) Dallas	48
Saint Louis	48
Toledo	48
39. (tie) Allentown	46
Buffalo	46
Honolulu	46
Louisville	46
Milwaukee	46
44. Minneapolis	45
45. (tie) Philadelphia	44
Syracuse	44
Tucson	44
48. Cleveland	43
49. Phoenix	42
50. (tie) Birmingham	41
New Orleans	41
52. Baltimore	40

Metro Area	Points
C–	
53. Columbus	38
54. Grand Rapids	37
55. (tie) Charleston	35
Cincinnati	35
57. (tie) Memphis	34
Sacramento	34
D+	
59. (tie) Chicago	32
San Diego	32
D	
61. (tie) Detroit	31
Norfolk	31
63. (tie) Baton Rouge	30
Dayton	30
Los Angeles	30
66. San Antonio	29
D–	
67. Rochester	28
68. Houston	27
F	
69. Las Vegas	22
70. Fresno	21
71. Salt Lake City	17
72. Bakersfield	7
73. El Paso	0

Test No. 5: Real Estate Opportunities

Pittsburgh and Honolulu don't have much in common. The gap between the two metro areas is every bit as wide as the 4,650-mile trip from the Golden Triangle to Waikiki Beach.

No kidding, you say. Everybody knows that Pittsburgh is a snowbound, rusting steel city and Honolulu is a warm, exciting island paradise. Who could possibly expect them to be similar in any way?

You might even be tempted to stretch the point by calling Pittsburgh a relic of America's industrial past and Honolulu a symbol of our future.

That would be terrible news for home buyers.

The truth is that Pittsburgh, described by its own mayor at the end of World War II as "the dirtiest slag pile in the United States," has undergone a remarkable renaissance. The 1985 edition of the *Places Rated Almanac* concluded that Pittsburgh was the best place to live in all of America.

Honolulu, ranked 63rd in the same book, has its drawbacks. Over-crowding is a big one, as we saw on the future growth test. The only areas with higher population densities than Honolulu are Boston, Chicago, and New York City.

But the most striking difference between the city of snow and steel and the city of sun-and-sand is in the cost of real estate.

• The typical single-family house in the Pittsburgh area was valued at $55,010 in 1990, according to the U.S. Census Bureau.

• The same home in Honolulu sold for $283,600 in 1990, roughly five times the Pittsburgh price.

The first component of the real estate opportunities test is a comparison of housing prices and income levels. The median value of a house in the Pittsburgh metro ($55,010) is 3.15 times larger than the annual per capita income of area residents ($17,455). That means the typical house in the Pittsburgh area costs $315 for every $100 of income, which is the most affordable ratio in the country.

"We're a conservative consuming market, anyway, so people are careful about big purchases," says Laurel McAdams, president of the Realtors Association of Metropolitan Pittsburgh. "There is a lot more realism here about property values. We did not have that dramatic upward spike in the late '80s that so many other markets did."

They know all about that upward spike in Honolulu, where real estate prices doubled between 1987 and 1990. The average Honolulu house costs $1,479 per $100 of income, which is the most lopsided ratio found in any metro.

"We have a different market out here than anywhere on the mainland," says Harvey Shapiro, research director of the Honolulu Board of Realtors.

70 "We have a shortage of housing, a very bad scarcity of land. We went through a major expansion in prices in the late 1980s, so affordability is quite low."

Look to the heartland for reasonably priced homes. Following Pittsburgh at the top of the housing costs component are Louisville, Oklahoma City, Omaha, and Detroit, all landlocked areas. Honolulu's companions at the bottom—San Francisco, Los Angeles, San Diego, and New York City—are ocean ports.

"It's partially a question of land constraints," says John Tuccillo, chief economist of the National Association of Realtors. "Those coastal cities don't have a lot of expansion room, so there is no low-cost way to meet demand with new housing. Besides, in the Midwest and South, costs are generally lower for labor and land than they are on either coast."

The regional focus narrows when it comes to property taxes, this test's second component. All ten metro areas with the lowest taxes—and hence the highest scores—are in the South.

The smallest levy is found in the Birmingham area, where the annual property tax load is just $168 per person. Nor is it likely to increase much in the future, since Alabama's constitution places tight limits on tax rates. Too tight, in the opinion of Ira Harvey, director of budget development at the University of Alabama-Birmingham.

"We have made the state safe for home ownership, but at the same time, we're strangling (tax) support for schools," says Harvey. "The property tax is too low; it should go up. But even when it does, it will still be extremely reasonable."

Baton Rouge, New Orleans, Little Rock, and Louisville have tax rates that are only slightly higher than Birmingham's. Each collects less than $253 per person per year.

But tax bills get substantially higher as you go north, peaking in the New York City area, where the property tax levy works out to a per capita figure of $901.

State policy seems to be the best explanation for New York City's tax woes. New York state's four other major metros—Albany, Buffalo, Rochester, and Syracuse—also are among the 20 areas with the highest property taxes in the country.

"Why are property taxes high in New York? Our conclusion is that it is the result of state mandates. The state [government] has shifted much of its financial burden on to local governments, and the property tax is the biggest local source of revenue," says Kent Gardner, director of economic analysis at the Center for Governmental Research in Rochester.

New York City is joined at the high end of the property tax scale by two New England areas, Hartford and New Haven, and two Southern metros, Houston and West Palm Beach.

The A+ metro area for real estate opportunities. Birmingham earned **71** the top score on this test by combining the nation's lowest property taxes with a very reasonably priced housing stock. The typical home in Birmingham is valued at $377 for every $100 of income, which is good for 12th place in the housing costs component.

"We are an undiscovered treasure," says Harvey. "Birmingham is a gorgeous city. Housing is relatively cheap. And once you get in it, you can afford to live in it."

The South swept the A range on this test. Louisville, Little Rock, Oklahoma City, Baton Rouge, and Knoxville received straight A's, while Tulsa and New Orleans were given grades of A–.

Metro Area	Points	Housing Costs Per $100 of Income
1. Pittsburgh	(100)	$315
2. Louisville	(97)	$340
3. Oklahoma City	(96)	$347
4. Omaha	(95)	$352
5. Detroit	(95)	$353
6. Toledo	(95)	$356
7. (tie) Houston	(94)	$363
Tulsa	(94)	$363
9. (tie) Kansas City	(93)	$371
Saint Louis	(93)	$371
11. Indianapolis	(92)	$376
12. Birmingham	(92)	$377
13. Little Rock	(92)	$380
14. Dayton	(91)	$386
15. (tie) Cleveland	(91)	$388
Greenville	(91)	$388
17. Richmond	(90)	$391
18. Memphis	(90)	$393
19. Grand Rapids	(90)	$394
20. Knoxville	(89)	$397
21. (tie) Greensboro	(89)	$402
Tampa	(89)	$402
23. Milwaukee	(89)	$403
24. West Palm Beach	(88)	$405
25. San Antonio	(88)	$407
26. Cincinnati	(88)	$411
27. Buffalo	(87)	$412
28. Portland	(87)	$415
29. Charlotte	(87)	$418
30. Dallas	(86)	$421

Metro Area	Points	Housing Costs Per $100 of Income
31. Columbus	(86)	$422
32. Jacksonville	(86)	$425
33. Rochester	(85)	$428
34. Minneapolis	(84)	$437
35. (tie) Scranton	(84)	$438
Syracuse	(84)	$438
37. Baton Rouge	(83)	$446
38. Harrisburg	(83)	$448
39. Miami	(82)	$456
40. (tie) Denver	(81)	$461
Nashville	(81)	$461
42. Atlanta	(80)	$472
43. (tie) New Orleans	(79)	$477
Orlando	(79)	$477
45. Austin	(79)	$480
46. Phoenix	(78)	$482
47. Raleigh	(78)	$489
48. Tucson	(76)	$503
49. Las Vegas	(76)	$504
50. Salt Lake City	(75)	$508
51. Baltimore	(75)	$511
52. Chicago	(74)	$516
53. Fresno	(73)	$525
54. Philadelphia	(73)	$527
55. Albany	(72)	$531
56. El Paso	(72)	$534
57. (tie) Bakersfield	(69)	$557
Norfolk	(69)	$557
59. Allentown	(68)	$564
60. Charleston	(65)	$586

Metro Area	Points	Housing Costs Per $100 of Income
61. Seattle	(59)	$631
62. Springfield	(53)	$680
63. Washington	(52)	$690
64. Hartford	(48)	$715
65. Providence	(46)	$735
66. Sacramento	(43)	$756
67. Boston	(43)	$757
68. New Haven	(43)	$760
69. New York City	(28)	$870
70. San Diego	(11)	$1,001
71. Los Angeles	(3)	$1,063
72. San Francisco	(0)	$1,089
73. Honolulu	(0)	$1,479

Metro Area	Points	Property Taxes Per Capita
1. Birmingham	(100)	$168
2. Baton Rouge	(95)	$201
3. New Orleans	(95)	$208
4. Little Rock	(91)	$233
5. Louisville	(89)	$252
6. Knoxville	(88)	$256
7. Oklahoma City	(86)	$273
8. El Paso	(83)	$295
9. Nashville	(83)	$296
10. Tulsa	(82)	$303
11. Honolulu	(80)	$311
12. Scranton	(80)	$318
13. Memphis	(79)	$322
14. Harrisburg	(78)	$327
15. (tie) Charleston	(77)	$335
Jacksonville	(77)	$335
17. Seattle	(77)	$336
18. (tie) Greensboro	(77)	$338
Greenville	(77)	$338
20. Las Vegas	(76)	$342
21. Saint Louis	(74)	$358
22. Norfolk	(72)	$374
23. Charlotte	(72)	$376
24. Fresno	(71)	$377
25. Kansas City	(71)	$381
26. Sacramento	(71)	$382
27. San Antonio	(70)	$387
28. Tampa	(70)	$389
29. (tie) Dayton	(69)	$397
Salt Lake City	(69)	$397
31. Toledo	(68)	$403

Metro Area	Points	Property Taxes Per Capita
32. Cincinnati	(68)	$405
33. (tie) Los Angeles	(67)	$412
Phoenix	(67)	$412
35. San Diego	(67)	$413
36. Baltimore	(66)	$414
37. Columbus	(66)	$420
38. Raleigh	(64)	$433
39. Orlando	(64)	$434
40. Indianapolis	(62)	$448
41. Richmond	(61)	$457
42. Springfield	(60)	$458
43. Allentown	(60)	$460
44. Atlanta	(55)	$498
45. Pittsburgh	(54)	$502
46. San Francisco	(54)	$506
47. Philadelphia	(53)	$513
48. Cleveland	(52)	$517
49. Tucson	(52)	$521
50. Miami	(46)	$562
51. Omaha	(43)	$586
52. Grand Rapids	(42)	$592
53. Dallas	(41)	$597
54. Albany	(41)	$602
55. Denver	(39)	$618
56. Chicago	(38)	$622
57. Bakersfield	(36)	$635
58. Buffalo	(36)	$637
59. Providence	(34)	$650
60. Rochester	(30)	$680
61. Washington	(29)	$685
62. Minneapolis	(29)	$687

Metro Area	Points	Property Taxes Per Capita
63. Austin	(29)	$688
64. Milwaukee	(28)	$698
65. Boston	(25)	$718
66. Detroit	(25)	$720
67. Portland	(24)	$727
68. Syracuse	(23)	$735
69. West Palm Beach	(20)	$758
70. New Haven	(18)	$766
71. Houston	(14)	$801
72. Hartford	(9)	$832
73. New York City	(0)	$901

Metro Area	Points
A+	
1. Birmingham	96
A	
2. Louisville	93
3. Little Rock	92
4. Oklahoma City	91
5. (tie) Baton Rouge	89
Knoxville	89
A–	
7. Tulsa	88
8. New Orleans	87
B+	
9. Memphis	85
10. (tie) Greenville	84
Saint Louis	84
B	
12. Greensboro	83
13. (tie) Jacksonville	82
Kansas City	82
Nashville	82
Scranton	82
Toledo	82
18. Harrisburg	81
19. (tie) Charlotte	80
Dayton	80
Tampa	80
22. San Antonio	79
B–	
23. (tie) Cincinnati	78
El Paso	78

Metro Area	Points
25. (tie) Indianapolis	77
Pittsburgh	77

C+

27. (tie) Columbus	76
Las Vegas	76
Richmond	76
30. Phoenix	73
31. (tie) Cleveland	72
Fresno	72
Orlando	72
Salt Lake City	72

C

35. (tie) Baltimore	71
Charleston	71
Norfolk	71
Raleigh	71
39. Omaha	69
40. (tie) Atlanta	68
Seattle	68
42. Grand Rapids	66
43. (tie) Allentown	64
Dallas	64
Miami	64
Tucson	64
47. Philadelphia	63
48. Buffalo	62
49. (tie) Denver	60
Detroit	60
51. Milwaukee	59
52. Rochester	58

Metro Area	Points
53. (tie) Albany	57
Minneapolis	57
Sacramento	57
Springfield	57
C–	
57. (tie) Chicago	56
Portland	56
59. (tie) Austin	54
Houston	54
Syracuse	54
West Palm Beach	54
63. Bakersfield	53
D+	
64. Washington	41
D	
65. (tie) Honolulu	40
Providence	40
67. San Diego	39
D–	
68. Los Angeles	35
69. Boston	34
F	
70. New Haven	31
71. Hartford	29
72. San Francisco	27
73. New York City	14

Test No. 6: Equality of Opportunities

Gail Turner faced a scary decision in 1985. At least it would have been scary to most of us.

Turner was comfortable as a staff assistant at Meetings & Management, a convention planning firm in the Denver suburb of Boulder, Colorado. But she suddenly was confronted by the prospect of change. Her boss had decided to sell the company.

Turner, with no experience in owning or operating a small business, didn't hesitate. She bought it.

"It's just the Western free spirit, I guess," she says. "People are more open out here. You don't have to follow rules as much. That makes you a bit more adventurous. Maybe that's why I never thought about failing. It never entered my mind."

Turner says her confidence has been rewarded. She and her two employees have all the business they can handle.

Turner's story is not an unusual one in Colorado. The first component of the equality of opportunities test gauges the progress of female entrepreneurs in each area, comparing the number of woman-owned businesses to the area's population. Denver has a ratio of 2,896 companies owned by women for every 100,000 residents, earning it the nation's top score.

Charlotte Redden, women's business coordinator for the Colorado Office of Business Development, agrees with Turner that geography deserves much of the credit for Denver's record.

"I think women do well here largely because we're in the West," says Redden. "We are not as class-bound or tradition-bound as other places, and that leads to more opportunities for everyone."

The rankings support her contention. The five best metros for women in business are in the West or Southwest, with San Francisco, Oklahoma City, Tulsa, and Austin joining Denver at the top.

The other end of the list is vastly different. El Paso holds last place, but seven other areas in the bottom ten are east of the Mississippi River.

The two halves of the country have opposite records in this component because their ways of thinking are not the same, says Jon Goodman, director of the entrepreneur program at the University of Southern California.

"In the West and Southwest, there is a fairly strong tradition of self-sufficiency among women. It may sound simplistic, but a certain amount of it is the frontier mentality," Goodman says. "The older, more established parts of the country have older, more established traditions of family and business. You don't find those in the West and Southwest, which makes it easier for women to advance."

You might expect that this open attitude also would make it easier for minority-group members to go into business. And it does, as reflected by the scores in this test's second component, which compares the number of minority-owned companies in an area to its total minority population.

It turns out that seven of the ten best areas for minorities in business are in the West or Southwest, with Honolulu at the top of the list. Honolulu admittedly is a special case. Marsha Anderson says minorities do so well there because the area has no *majority* group.

"What's a minority in Hawaii? Everyone is a minority," says Anderson, a spokeswoman for the Hawaii Department of Business, Economic Development, and Tourism. "We're about one-third Caucasian, one-third Japanese, and smaller chunks of Chinese and Filipino heritage. We have quite a hodgepodge."

The U.S. Census Bureau, which uses the same classifications in Hawaii as on the mainland, says that about 70 percent of Honolulu's residents are minorities. But they aren't minorities in a local sense. Hawaiians of Asian heritage outnumber whites by a 2–1 margin.

That's a major reason why Honolulu has an impressive ratio of 43.3 minority-owned companies for every 1,000 minority residents. Miami, San Francisco, Washington, and Denver round out the top five.

These areas share one important quality. Their minority groups are large enough that they can wield substantial clout in business. Minorities account for 52 percent of the population in the Miami area, which has a politically influential Hispanic community, while 39 percent of the residents of the San Francisco area are members of minority groups.

Ken Sacharin, media director of the advertising agency of Young & Rubicam in San Francisco, says that his city's large Asian population has energized the local economy.

"Speaking broadly, Asians are known for their tremendous work ethic," Sacharin says. "They want to achieve economic success, and they do. Asians have the highest household income of any group in the country, including Caucasians."

There are some familiar names at the bottom of the minority-owned business list. Last-place Birmingham and next-to-last Buffalo also are among the six worst areas for women.

"Prejudice is running rampant here," says Diane White, president of Professional Data Communications, a Buffalo computer training firm. "People will look at my skin color [she is black] and just tune me out before ever listening to what I say. The men here are very conservative, very closed."

The conventional wisdom is that no region could possibly be more discouraging to minorities in business than the South. Don't believe it. The reality is that the East dominates the bottom of the list, with five of the ten worst scores. Three others are from the Midwest; only two are in the South.

The A+ metro area for equality of opportunities. San Francisco, well known for its free and easy outlook on life, finished first on this test. It had outstanding scores in both components, ranking second in the nation for women in business and third for minorities.

"It's all demographics," says Sacharin. "San Francisco is one of the most ethnically diverse cities in the country. There's a large Asian community, a large black community, and a large Hispanic community. People here have had to learn to work together."

The West clearly outperformed other regions on this test, taking five of the seven slots in the A range. Denver and Honolulu received straight A's, while Portland and Seattle were awarded grades of A–. The two non-Western areas at the top were Miami (A) and Washington (A–).

Woman-Owned Businesses: Top to Bottom

Metro Area	Points	Woman-Owned Businesses Per 100,000 Residents
1. Denver	(100)	2,896
2. San Francisco	(100)	2,333
3. Oklahoma City	(89)	2,210
4. Tulsa	(87)	2,190
5. Austin	(86)	2,173
6. West Palm Beach	(82)	2,129
7. Minneapolis	(82)	2,128
8. Portland	(78)	2,088
9. Dallas	(77)	2,070
10. Seattle	(74)	2,038
11. Washington	(71)	2,007
12. Boston	(68)	1,970
13. Kansas City	(64)	1,930
14. San Diego	(62)	1,900
15. Honolulu	(58)	1,863
16. Miami	(55)	1,821
17. Sacramento	(55)	1,819
18. Los Angeles	(54)	1,816
19. Salt Lake City	(54)	1,810
20. Houston	(52)	1,792
21. Indianapolis	(51)	1,774
22. Nashville	(50)	1,770
23. Phoenix	(50)	1,763
24. Atlanta	(48)	1,741
25. Raleigh	(47)	1,733
26. Omaha	(46)	1,727
27. Tucson	(45)	1,714
28. Tampa	(44)	1,703
29. Louisville	(42)	1,681
30. New York City	(41)	1,670

Metro Area	Points	Woman-Owned Businesses Per 100,000 Residents
31. Little Rock	(41)	1,663
32. Hartford	(40)	1,651
33. Orlando	(38)	1,629
34. Columbus	(37)	1,626
35. Saint Louis	(35)	1,598
36. Greensboro	(35)	1,595
37. New Haven	(32)	1,563
38. Baltimore	(31)	1,549
39. Rochester	(30)	1,546
40. Grand Rapids	(29)	1,529
41. Knoxville	(28)	1,522
42. Harrisburg	(28)	1,519
43. San Antonio	(28)	1,514
44. Springfield	(26)	1,493
45. Albany	(25)	1,486
46. Baton Rouge	(24)	1,473
47. Dayton	(22)	1,455
48. Chicago	(22)	1,453
49. (tie) Allentown	(22)	1,452
New Orleans	(22)	1,452
51. Syracuse	(18)	1,402
52. Cincinnati	(18)	1,401
53. Philadelphia	(17)	1,396
54. (tie) Cleveland	(17)	1,392
Providence	(17)	1,392
56. Charlotte	(17)	1,390
57. Scranton	(16)	1,389
58. Detroit	(16)	1,384
59. Jacksonville	(16)	1,382
60. Las Vegas	(13)	1,347

Metro Area	Points	Woman-Owned Businesses Per 100,000 Residents
61. Richmond	(12)	1,344
62. Toledo	(12)	1,336
63. Charleston	(12)	1,335
64. Pittsburgh	(11)	1,326
65. Milwaukee	(10)	1,320
66. Greenville	(7)	1,285
67. Bakersfield	(7)	1,282
68. Birmingham	(5)	1,259
69. Norfolk	(4)	1;249
70. Memphis	(2)	1,226
71. Fresno	(0)	1,205
72. Buffalo	(0)	1,203
73. El Paso	(0)	949

Metro Area	Points	Minority-Owned Businesses Per 1,000 Minority Residents
1. Honolulu	(100)	43.3
2. Miami	(100)	38.5
3. San Francisco	(75)	31.4
4. Washington	(60)	27.0
5. Denver	(59)	26.7
6. Los Angeles	(57)	26.3
7. Houston	(55)	25.7
8. Seattle	(55)	25.6
9. Portland	(54)	25.5
10. Scranton	(54)	25.4
11. San Antonio	(51)	24.5
12. Tampa	(49)	24.1
13. Dallas	(46)	23.2
14. Sacramento	(46)	23.1
15. (tie) San Diego	(44)	22.5
West Palm Beach	(44)	22.5
17. Austin	(41)	21.6
18. El Paso	(35)	20.1
19. Salt Lake City	(34)	19.8
20. Nashville	(34)	19.6
21. Orlando	(33)	19.5
22. Atlanta	(32)	19.2
23. New York City	(32)	19.0
24. Raleigh	(31)	18.7
25. Knoxville	(29)	18.3
26. Columbus	(29)	18.2
27. (tie) Indianapolis	(27)	17.8
Richmond	(27)	17.8
29. New Orleans	(27)	17.7
30. Kansas City	(27)	17.6

Metro Area	Points	Minority-Owned Businesses Per 1,000 Minority Residents
31. Oklahoma City	(26)	17.3
32. Baltimore	(25)	17.2
33. Harrisburg	(25)	17.0
34. (tie) Albany	(24)	16.9
Allentown	(24)	16.9
36. Louisville	(24)	16.8
37. Tulsa	(23)	16.5
38. Minneapolis	(22)	16.4
39. Cincinnati	(22)	16.3
40. Saint Louis	(22)	16.2
41. (tie) Bakersfield	(21)	16.1
Pittsburgh	(21)	16.1
43. Boston	(21)	16.0
44. (tie) Baton Rouge	(20)	15.8
Tucson	(20)	15.8
46. Omaha	(20)	15.7
47. (tie) Dayton	(20)	15.6
Phoenix	(20)	15.6
49. Little Rock	(19)	15.5
50. Greensboro	(19)	15.4
51. Norfolk	(19)	15.3
52. Las Vegas	(18)	15.2
53. (tie) Chicago	(18)	15.1
Cleveland	(18)	15.1
55. (tie) Fresno	(17)	14.8
Jacksonville	(17)	14.8
57. Philadelphia	(16)	14.7
58. Charlotte	(16)	14.6
59. New Haven	(14)	14.0
60. Syracuse	(14)	13.9

Metro Area	Points	Minority-Owned Businesses Per 1,000 Minority Residents
61. Charleston	(13)	13.7
62. Memphis	(12)	13.4
63. Detroit	(11)	13.2
64. Toledo	(11)	13.0
65. Providence	(10)	12.9
66. Hartford	(10)	12.8
67. Rochester	(9)	12.7
68. Greenville	(7)	12.1
69. Grand Rapids	(4)	11.1
70. Springfield	(4)	11.0
71. Milwaukee	(3)	10.9
72. Buffalo	(1)	10.4
73. Birmingham	(0)	10.0

Equality of Opportunities: Scores and Grades

Metro Area		Points
	A+	
1. San Francisco		88
	A	
2. Denver		80
3. Honolulu		79
4. Miami		78
	A–	
5. (tie) Portland		66
Washington		66
7. Seattle		65
	B+	
8. Austin		64
9. West Palm Beach		63
10. Dallas		62
	B	
11. Oklahoma City		58
12. Los Angeles		56
13. Tulsa		55
14. Houston		54
15. San Diego		53
16. Minneapolis		52
17. Sacramento		51
18. Tampa		47
19. Kansas City		46
20. Boston		45
21. Salt Lake City		44
22. Nashville		42
	B–	
23. (tie) Atlanta		40
San Antonio		40

Metro Area	Points
25. (tie) Indianapolis	39
Raleigh	39

―――――――――― C+ ――――――――――

27. New York City	37
28. Orlando	36
29. (tie) Phoenix	35
Scranton	35

―――――――――― C ――――――――――

31. (tie) Columbus	33
Louisville	33
Omaha	33
Tucson	33
35. Little Rock	30
36. (tie) Knoxville	29
Saint Louis	29
38. Baltimore	28
39. (tie) Greensboro	27
Harrisburg	27
41. (tie) Albany	25
Hartford	25
New Orleans	25
44. (tie) Allentown	23
New Haven	23
46. Baton Rouge	22
47. Dayton	21
48. (tie) Chicago	20
Cincinnati	20
Richmond	20
Rochester	20

Metro Area	Points
C–	
52. (tie) Cleveland	18
El Paso	18
54. (tie) Charlotte	17
Grand Rapids	17
Jacksonville	17
Philadelphia	17
D+	
58. (tie) Las Vegas	16
Pittsburgh	16
Syracuse	16
D	
61. Springfield	15
62. (tie) Bakersfield	14
Detroit	14
Providence	14
65. Charleston	13
D–	
66. (tie) Norfolk	12
Toledo	12
F	
68. Fresno	9
69. (tie) Greenville	7
Memphis	7
Milwaukee	7
72. Birmingham	3
73. Buffalo	1

2

The Final Results

Every school year, no matter how long it might drag on, eventually reaches an end. There can be only so many tests. Then it comes time for the teacher to conduct a final assessment, total up the year's scores, and enter each student's final grade on his or her report card.

We have reached that point in our examination of America's 73 largest metropolitan areas. The previous chapter subjected each of these places to six rigorous tests. We noted and analyzed the results. Now we must assess each metro area's overall performance, calculate its total score, and award its final grade.

Keep in mind that our aim is a narrow one. We are not delving into all of the factors that determine a place's quality of life; we are merely searching for the metro areas that offer the best and broadest ranges of economic opportunities. Let's take another look at the profile of our ideal area:

- It registered strong increases in population and per capita income during the 1980s.
- It will continue to expand at an impressive pace through the 1990s

94 and well into the next century, and it has enough space to easily accommodate this additional growth.

• It has a rapidly expanding job base, coupled with a low unemployment rate.

• It welcomes the establishment of new businesses, particularly in the retail and service sectors.

• It has affordable real estate and low property taxes.

• It extends economic opportunities to all people, regardless of gender or race.

We already know that this ideal place does not exist. Not one of the 73 metro areas managed to pull straight A's on all six tests; every region has its rough edges, its economic faults. So it becomes a question of degree. Which area comes closest to our ideal? Which has the largest array of positive qualities, along with the fewest negatives? Which area, in short, offers the best opportunities to make money?

And the answer is . . . West Palm Beach, a rapidly growing metro area on Florida's Atlantic coast, about 70 miles north of Miami. West Palm Beach earned the nation's highest total score, 820 points. It is the only metro to be awarded an overall grade of A+ for the excellence of its economic climate.

But don't call for the moving van just yet. West Palm Beach is not the only place that deserves your attention. Six other areas received overall grades of A or A–. They join West Palm Beach on our list of Grade A metros: Orlando, Las Vegas, Raleigh, Seattle, Sacramento, and Phoenix. Nor should you ignore the other 66 areas, even though they received lower grades. Each has economic strong points that you might find appealing.

Your next step, then, should be to take a closer look at the final results. Learn why each metro area finished where it did. You can find the explanations in the rest of this chapter, which is devoted to an area-by-area review of the scores and grades that you see in the chart. We will begin our cross-country trip at No. 1 West Palm Beach and go all the way to No. 73 El Paso.

Metro Area	Points
A+	
1. West Palm Beach	820
A	
2. Orlando	747
3. Las Vegas	730
4. Raleigh	692
5. Seattle	677
A–	
6. Sacramento	655
7. Phoenix	638
B+	
8. Knoxville	635
9. Tampa	634
10. Miami	632
11. Nashville	624
B	
12. Denver	614
13. San Diego	603
14. Atlanta	599
15. Portland	597
16. Jacksonville	595
17. Washington	585
18. San Francisco	584
19. Richmond	578
20. Charlotte	575
21. Greensboro	565
B–	
22. (tic) Indianapolis	560
Little Rock	560
24. (tie) Honolulu	558
Tucson	558

Metro Area	Points
C+	
26. Kansas City	543
27. (tie) Austin	533
Tulsa	533
29. Minneapolis	527
30. Oklahoma City	523
31. (tie) Los Angeles	522
Scranton	522
C	
33. Louisville	520
34. (tie) Greenville	514
Harrisburg	514
36. Dallas	508
37. Columbus	507
38. Omaha	506
39. (tie) Baltimore	502
Birmingham	502
41. Memphis	498
42. Albany	493
43. Saint Louis	489
44. Grand Rapids	488
45. Salt Lake City	484
46. Hartford	471
47. Allentown	467
48. Springfield	466
49. Charleston	464
50. Fresno	462
51. Boston	451

Metro Area	Points
C–	
52. (tie)　Cincinnati	447
Norfolk	447
San Antonio	447
55.　Philadelphia	436
56.　Syracuse	430
57.　New Haven	429
58.　Toledo	426
D+	
59. (tie)　Pittsburgh	423
Rochester	423
D	
61.　Providence	420
62.　Dayton	417
63.　Bakersfield	410
64.　Houston	408
65.　Baton Rouge	391
66.　Cleveland	383
D–	
67.　New York City	381
68.　Milwaukee	380
69.　Buffalo	370
F	
70.　Detroit	360
71.　New Orleans	355
72.　Chicago	352
73.　El Paso	346

98 Scoring

There is always a point during the Academy Awards when two accountants shuffle on stage. They ramble on and on about the arcane rules that determine who wins that year's Oscars. The show instantly loses the small amount of pacing and suspense that it had.

We have come to that point of this book. Read on if you really want to know how each metro's overall score was calculated. (We're going to tell you in mind-numbing detail.) Skip to the next subheading if you really don't care.

There are two ways to explain this calculation. Our first option is to dazzle (or bore) you with algebra:

$$TP=2(EM)+2(FG)+1.5(JO)+1.5(BO)+1.5(REO)+1.5(EOO)+(CGB)+(GPB)+(ETB)$$

Or we could use simple English. Let's take Las Vegas as an example, going step by step through the formula to figure out its score. Las Vegas' total points **(TP)** equal the sum of the following:

- **2(EM).** Multiply the *economic momentum* score by two. Las Vegas received 94 points on this test. That's 188 points when doubled.
- **2(FG).** Multiply the *future growth* score by two. Las Vegas' 93 points turn into 186 for the purposes of this formula.
- **1.5(JO).** Multiply the *job opportunities* score by 1.5. Las Vegas' 80 points become 120.
- **1.5(BO).** Multiply the *business opportunities* score by 1.5. Las Vegas' 22 points equal 33.
- **1.5(REO).** Multiply the *real estate opportunities* score by 1.5. The score for Las Vegas increases from 76 points to 114.
- **1.5(EEO).** Multiply the *equality of opportunities* score by 1.5. Las Vegas' 16 points turn into 24.
- **(CGB).** A *category grade bonus* is awarded for each grade of A- or better on the six tests. Metros receive 20 bonus points for each A+, 15 for each A, and 10 for each A-. Las Vegas totals 55 bonus points for an A+ for economic momentum, another A+ for future growth, and a straight A for job opportunities.
- **(GPB).** A *growth potential bonus* of five points is awarded if the metro has one or more counties with growth potential scores of A- or better. (The concept of growth potential will be explained in the next chapter.) The bonus totals five points no matter how many counties meet this standard. The Las Vegas area receives the bonus because Clark County, Nevada, has a growth potential grade of A-.
- **(ETB).** An *employment trends bonus* of five points is awarded if six or seven of the metro's major employment sectors are rated hot. (Em-

ployment sector ratings are also explained in the next chapter.) All seven sectors are hot in Las Vegas, earning it five points.

Add it all up, and Las Vegas receives a total score of 730 points. But that's only half of the process. There still is the matter of coming up with a final grade.

Grading an area, you'll be glad to hear, is much easier than figuring out its score. We use a simple curve, just as we did when we graded each of the tests. (The curve is explained in the previous chapter.) The 73 metro areas are lined up in order of their total scores and are rewarded accordingly. Las Vegas is in third place, which earns it an A.

Overall grades are directly tied to total scores; they are not connected in any way to an area's grades on the six tests. That's why Detroit has an overall grade of F, even though it received two C's and four D's on the tests. Detroit's total score of 360 points puts it in 70th place. Only three metros did worse.

So there you have it: an inside look at how we scored and graded the economic opportunities in each metro area. Now, on with the countdown.

Grade A Metros

1. West Palm Beach

Population: 863,518
Overall Grade: A+

West Palm Beach was designed to play a subordinate role. Developer Henry Flagler built two magnificent resort hotels around the turn of the century, including the famed Breakers, that transformed Palm Beach into a playground for the rich. Palm Beach badly needed a supply center, as well as a terminal to serve the private railway cars of the wealthy. Thus was born West Palm Beach. Flagler always said he built it "for my help."

The rich still flock to Palm Beach, but it is middle-class West Palm Beach that has become demographically dominant, the center of the metropolitan area that offers the best economic opportunities in America. The area is expected to have more than 1 million residents by 2000. It has become a thriving high-technology center and also has a large number of retirees, who can be found in suburbs such as Delray Beach and Boynton Beach.

No American metro is growing as rapidly as West Palm Beach. Its population jumped nearly 50 percent between 1980 and 1990, and demographers predict an additional 46 percent increase by 2020. West Palm Beach received the nation's highest score in the business opportunities test. It has the healthiest retail sector in the country; only Denver has a stronger service sector. The area's worst grade was a C– for real estate opportunities. Housing is generally affordable—outside of Palm Beach—but property taxes are among the highest in the country.

2. Orlando

Population: 1,072,748
Overall Grade: A

Orlando defied geography in becoming one of 38 metros in America with more than 1 million residents. It is landlocked in a state where growth has always been concentrated near beaches and ports. The Orlando area consequently had only 453,000 residents as late as 1970. But the area's history has been marked by timely pushes that allowed it to build up economic momentum. First there was the rise of the citrus industry; then the arrival of aerospace companies attracted by Orlando's proximity to Cape Canaveral; and, finally, the construction of Walt Disney World, one of the country's premier tourist magnets.

Orlando grew an astonishing 53 percent during the 1980s. The pace will slow in coming years, but the area's population still is expected to increase another 35 percent by 2020. Many new residents are lured by the expanding job base. Orlando's unemployment rate historically is below the national average, and the area received the country's highest score on the job opportunities test.

3. Las Vegas

Population: 741,459
Overall Grade: A

Las Vegas is one of the country's amazing growth stories. It was founded by the Mormons as a desert mission in the mid-1800s and remained a sleepy town well into this century. The city had only 8,400 residents in 1940. Gambling was legalized in Nevada in 1931, but Reno quickly became the state's center for games of chance. It seemed unlikely that Las Vegas could ever catch up. But catch up it did. Las Vegas now is acknowledged to be the national capital of legalized gambling, epitomized by the gaudy, wildly flashing signs of its famous Strip.

Rapid expansion will continue to be the rule in Las Vegas. The area received grades of A+ for economic momentum and future growth. Its population is projected to increase by 40 percent between 1990 and 2020. Jobs naturally are plentiful in such an environment. But Las Vegas does have a few economic drawbacks. Its retail and service sectors are relatively weak, and it has a poor record of extending business opportunities to women and minorities.

4. Raleigh

Population: 735,480
Overall Grade: A

The Raleigh area is known in North Carolina as the Research Triangle. The first word in the regional name explicitly recognizes the importance of education and high technology to the local economy. The second word is an admission that Raleigh is not the area's only prominent city. A major university can be found at each point of the Research Triangle: Raleigh (North Carolina State University), Durham (Duke University), and Chapel Hill (University of North Carolina).

Raleigh received straight A's on the job opportunities and business opportunities tests. The area has an impressive array of stable employers, beginning with the universities themselves. The laboratories and research facilities located in the Triangle have hired thousands of local college graduates. Raleigh is the capital of North Carolina, so the state government is another reliable source of jobs. The Raleigh area had an average annual unemployment rate of 2.8 percent between 1985 and 1990. No other metro did better.

5. Seattle

Population: 2,559,164
Overall Grade: A

Towering over downtown Seattle is the Space Needle, a remnant of the 1962 World's Fair at which Seattle boldly proclaimed itself to be the city of the future. It seemed destined to be an unfulfilled prophecy. Seattle's fortunes historically were linked to the performance of its largest employer, Boeing, the aerospace giant. Boeing—and Seattle—hit such heavy turbulence in the early 1970s that a few local wits rented billboard space to ask, "Will the last person out of Seattle please turn out the lights?"

Seattle's economy is more diversified today, and the area has emerged as a major commercial center, not just for the Pacific Northwest but for all of the West. Unemployment is relatively low. Seattle, in fact, received an A on the job opportunities test. Forecasts call for a population increase of nearly 25 percent by 2020, but Seattle residents no longer are as excited about expansion as they were during the World's Fair. They now worry publicly about becoming another Los Angeles and not-so-delicately refer to growth as "Californication."

6. Sacramento

Population: 1,481,102
Overall Grade: A–

California has become the dominant force in American politics. It holds 12 percent of all seats in the House of Representatives and is by far the biggest prize in each presidential election. Los Angeles and San Francisco are California's high-profile metros, but the real power in this nation-state belongs to its capital, Sacramento. Fully 29 percent of the Sacramento area's workers have government jobs.

Don't expect to find the one-dimensional economy that is common to many state capitals. Sacramento is the largest city and biggest agricultural center in California's Central Valley, and it also is a major inland port. The local unemployment rate tends to be lower than the national average.

Housing costs are high on a national scale, but they are considerably lower than those of nearby San Francisco. That is a key factor in attracting new residents to Sacramento. Demographers predict that the area's population will increase nearly 35 percent between 1990 and 2020. The fastest growth will occur in Placer County, northeast of the city, and El Dorado County, which is due east.

7. Phoenix

Population: 2,122,101
Overall Grade: A–

Phoenix is the metropolitan area that air conditioning built. The Valley of the Sun had only 65,000 residents in 1940, hardy souls who braved summer temperatures that daily topped 100 degrees. Anyone who at that time had predicted massive population growth would have been taken for a heat-stroke victim. But technological advances after World War II made it possible to efficiently cool homes, office buildings, and cars. Midwestern retirees, attracted by the area's low humidity and pleasant winter temperatures, began streaming to Phoenix. Real estate developers and electronics firms also set up shop, enticed by the area's pro-growth attitude and relatively low taxes.

There seem to be few limits on how large Phoenix can get, as long as it has enough water and electricity to power its air conditioners. The Phoenix metro has more than 2 million residents, yet its population density still is among the lowest in the country. The area is expected to grow another 42 percent by 2020, putting it above the 3 million mark.

Better than Average

8. Knoxville

Population: 604,816
Overall Grade: B+

Knoxville often surpasses what people expect of a medium-sized Southern metro. That certainly was the case when it was selected as the site of the 1982 World's Fair. It also is true in this book, where Knoxville has the highest score of any metro with fewer than 700,000 residents. The area received straight A's on the business opportunities and real estate opportunities tests. Knoxville is home to the Tennessee Valley Authority and the University of Tennessee; the government sector accounts for one out of every five jobs.

9. Tampa

Population: 2,067,959
Overall Grade: B+

Tampa is a center for brewing, cigar making, shipbuilding, and steel production, all of which give it the feel of a Northern industrial city. Across Tampa Bay is the area's other large city, Saint Petersburg, which has long been a retirement haven for Midwesterners. Both sides of the bay have diversified in the past quarter-century: Tampa now has a strong tourism sector, while Saint Petersburg is going after research and development firms. The Tampa area has a remarkably consistent record in terms of economic opportunities. It received straight B's on all six tests. Also of note is the exceptional growth potential of Hernando County, located on the northern fringe of the metro area.

10. Miami

Population: 3,192,582
Overall Grade: B+

Miami was a boom town during the 1980s, emerging as a major center for America's increasingly important trade with Latin America. But future growth is expected to be only slightly above the national average, and the

104 key question is where to put everybody. Miami is one of the most congested metros in the country. The local economy has two remarkable strengths: only West Palm Beach outscored Miami on the business opportunities test. And the area received an A for equality of opportunities, evidence of the clout wielded by Miami's large Hispanic, black, and Jewish communities.

11. Nashville

Population: 985,026
Overall Grade: B+

Nashville earned an overall grade of B+ with a consistent performance, scoring in the B range on all six tests. The area is best known as the home of country music, but the stability of its job market actually can be traced to the presence of the state government. The local unemployment rate is consistently below the national average. Nashville is expected to continue expanding at a rapid pace, with future growth being focused south of the city in Rutherford and Williamson counties.

12. Denver

Population: 1,848,319
Overall Grade: B

Denver struggled during the energy bust of the 1980s, but its future will be brighter. The area's population is expected to increase 32 percent between 1990 and 2020; only eight metros have higher projected growth rates. Another plus is the relative ease with which women and minority entrepreneurs are welcomed to the business community. Future growth will be strongest in Douglas County, located between Denver and Colorado Springs on Interstate 25.

13. San Diego

Population: 2,498,016
Overall Grade: B

First there was one of the continent's best natural harbors; then came San Diego. It was almost inevitable that the harbor would attract the navy, which in turn would become a major component of the local economy. Military aircraft manufacturers also established themselves before World War II. San Diego consequently prospered or suffered depending on the size of the military budget, but it has diversified its economy over the past half-century. The area received a straight A for job opportunities. The biggest local problem is real estate, which is very expensive by national standards.

14. Atlanta

Population: 2,833,511
Overall Grade: B

Atlanta's successful bid to host the 1996 Summer Olympics is evidence that this economic center of the Southeast is transforming itself into a world city. Nor are the suburbs being left behind. Several suburban counties, notably Fayette and Gwinnett, are among the nation's leaders in growth potential. Jobs are plentiful, particularly in the rapidly expanding service sector. The Atlanta area's lowest grade was a straight C on the real estate opportunities test.

15. Portland

Population: 1,477,895
Overall Grade: B

Portland is ideally located to fill a geographic void. It is the only major metropolitan area between Seattle and San Francisco, and consequently has developed into an important regional banking, legal, and business center. Portland is projected to expand at a healthy rate of 23 percent between 1990 and 2020. Future growth will be concentrated west of the city in Washington County and north of the Columbia River in Clark County, Washington. The area's highest grade was an A– in the equality of opportunities test.

16. Jacksonville

Population: 906,727
Overall Grade: B

Tourism is the economic engine in most Florida metros, but not in Jacksonville. Out-of-state visitors usually are drawn farther south by beaches and other attractions. Jacksonville, isolated in the northeastern corner of Florida, concentrated on developing a major port, attracting military installations, and becoming a regional insurance center. The strategy has worked well. The Jacksonville area is expected to grow 35 percent between 1990 and 2020. Clay and Saint Johns counties, both south of the city, will lead the way.

17. Washington, D.C.

Population: 3,923,574
Overall Grade: B

The federal government, of course, historically has been the largest employer in the Washington area. At least that was true until the 1980s, when service

106 industries took the lead. The gap between the two already is substantial. The service sector now accounts for 34 percent of all employment, while government is at 26 percent. Jobs always seem to be plentiful; only Raleigh had a lower annual unemployment rate between 1985 and 1990. Future growth will be concentrated on the outskirts of this far-flung metro, as home buyers try to escape high housing costs. The Washington area received a D+ on the real estate opportunities test.

18. San Francisco

Population: 6,253,311
Overall Grade: B

The San Francisco area brings together a wide array of sexual, ethnic, and racial groups that coexist remarkably well. San Francisco received the nation's highest grade on the equality of opportunities test. At the opposite end of the spectrum is the area's F for real estate opportunities; only Honolulu has higher housing costs. The metro includes three large cities—San Francisco, San Jose, and Oakland—but its future growth center will be relatively tiny Solano County, located on Interstate 80 between San Francisco and Sacramento.

19. Richmond

Population: 865,640
Overall Grade: B

Tradition counts for much in Virginia. That's good news for Richmond, which is only the third-largest city in the state, but remains its commercial and cultural center, partly because of its mystique as the capital of the old Confederacy. The area's population is projected to expand 25 percent between 1990 and 2020, with Chesterfield County having the strongest growth potential. Richmond's unemployment rate generally is one or two percentage points below the national average. Give credit to a diverse economy that ranges from tobacco processing to state government.

20. Charlotte

Population: 1,162,093
Overall Grade: B

Charlotte does not fit the usual pattern of a declining central city ringed by rapidly expanding suburbs. Mecklenburg County, which includes the city of Charlotte, outscores all of its suburban counties in terms of growth potential. The Charlotte area is one of the best places in the country to find work. The local unemployment rate is well below the national average. All sectors, including manufacturing, are adding jobs.

21. Greensboro

Population: 942,091
Overall Grade: B

Greensboro relies on industry more heavily than so-called Northern "smoke-stack" cities do. The manufacturing sector accounts for 30 percent of all jobs in the Greensboro area, compared to current figures of 23 percent in Detroit and 13 percent in Pittsburgh. But Greensboro has been able to avoid the economic volatility that characterizes other manufacturing centers. Its unemployment rate in recent years has stayed about two percentage points below the national average.

22. (tie) Indianapolis

Population: 1,249,822
Overall Grade: B–

Indianapolis has the image of being a staid, conservative, somewhat sleepy town. It actually ranks first in the Midwest in economic opportunities. Indianapolis has a strongly diversified economy, ranging from pharmaceutical industries to state government. Unemployment runs below the national rate. The area's population is expected to increase another 20 percent by 2020, with the fastest growth being seen north of the city in Hamilton County.

22. (tie) Little Rock

Population: 513,117
Overall Grade: B–

Little Rock is among the best places in America to buy real estate. Only three of the nation's major metros have property taxes lower than Little Rock's; only twelve have housing that is more affordable. The area also can be proud of its gains in extending business opportunities to others besides white men, though more progress is needed. Little Rock, once a stronghold of resistance to school desegregation, received a straight C on the equality of opportunities test.

24. (tie) Honolulu

Population: 836,231
Overall Grade: B–

Honolulu might have qualified as a Grade A metro, but for one thing: it is running out of room. The Honolulu area, confined to a single island of the Hawaiian archipelago, is more crowded than all metros except Boston, Chicago, and New York City. The result is the most expensive housing in the country. Honolulu's economy has two notable strengths: Unemployment is very low, and no area is more willing to extend business opportunities to members of minority groups.

24. (tie) Tucson

Population: 666,880
Overall Grade: B–

Tucson has been unable to match the growth rate of nearby Phoenix, but the area is by no means sluggish. Demographers expect Tucson's population to increase by an impressive 32 percent between 1990 and 2020, compared to the astronomical rate of 42 percent for Phoenix. Tucson is the home of the University of Arizona, which turns out an educated work force that has attracted several high-technology companies to the area.

Middle of the Pack

26. Kansas City

Population: 1,566,280
Overall Grade: C+

Kansas City, belying its cow town image, is one of the Midwest's most rapidly expanding areas. Its population is projected to increase 21 percent between 1990 and 2020. The focus of this growth is Johnson County, Kansas, one of the most prosperous suburban counties in the nation. Also working in Kansas City's favor is the fact that real estate is relatively inexpensive.

27. (tie) Austin

Population: 781,572
Overall Grade: C+

Austin, home of the University of Texas and the state government, is known as the most liberal city in Texas. The government sector remains the largest employer, but no longer is the sole pillar of the economy. Austin, in fact, is one of the few areas in the country where manufacturing is gaining strength. Look for population growth to be centered in Williamson County, a short drive north of the city on Interstate 35.

27. (tie) Tulsa

Population: 708,954
Overall Grade: C+

Tulsa began as an insignificant post office stop for the Pony Express. The discovery of oil in 1906 changed everything, transforming Tulsa into the self-proclaimed oil capital of the world. The boast rang hollow during the energy bust of the 1980s, which earned Tulsa an F on the economic momentum test. But conditions already are improving. Tulsa's economy has gradually diversified in recent decades, adding aeronautics industries and a deep-water port. The area's population is expected to increase 19 percent between 1990 and 2020.

29. Minneapolis

Population: 2,464,124
Overall Grade: C+

A nation of sports fanatics became well acquainted with Minneapolis in 1991–92, as the area pulled off the unprecedented feat of hosting hockey's Stanley Cup playoffs, baseball's World Series, football's Super Bowl, and college basketball's Final Four in a 12-month period. This televised bonanza is proof that the frosty Twin Cities area (don't forget Saint Paul) is working hard to promote itself as an alternative to the Sunbelt. The area's population is expected to grow by a healthy 21 percent between 1990 and 2020, a faster pace than Miami, Raleigh, or Charlotte, among others.

30. Oklahoma City

Population: 958,839
Overall Grade: C+

Oil was discovered under Oklahoma City in the 1930s and quickly became the driving force of the local economy. Tinker Air Force Base also is a large employer. Oklahoma City prospered as the petroleum and military sectors grew, but it learned tough lessons from the energy bust of the 1980s and the later threat of military cuts. Its economy now is more diversified. Oklahoma City's strength is its affordable real estate. Only Pittsburgh and Louisville have lower housing costs.

31. (tie) Los Angeles

Population: 14,531,529
Overall Grade: C+

The West's largest urban area also is one of its worst in terms of economic opportunities. Los Angeles ranks 11th among the fourteen Western metros. The negatives are easily listed: urban congestion, overpriced real estate, and a relatively weak retail sector. But Los Angeles will keep expanding. Demographers expect a population jump of 27 percent between 1990 and 2020. The county with the strongest growth potential is Riverside, east of the city.

31. (tie) Scranton

Population: 734,175
Overall Grade: C+

The Scranton area literally was built on anthracite coal. The mines once were a dependable source of jobs. But anthracite is expensive to extract, and few mine operators are willing to bother with it these days. Unemployment in Scranton consequently runs higher than the national average. But there also is good news. Housing costs are fairly reasonable, earning the Scranton area a B on the real estate opportunities test. And Monroe County, whose mountain resorts are southeast of the city, has strong growth potential.

33. Louisville

Population: 952,662
Overall Grade: C

Louisville rightfully can brag about its real estate. It finished second to Pittsburgh in the comparison of housing costs to per capita income, earning

a straight A on the real estate opportunities test. But there was a dull **111**
sameness to the other five tests: Louisville landed in the C range on all
of them. The only county with above-average growth potential is Oldham,
northeast of the city along the Ohio River.

34. (tie) Greenville

Population: 640,861
Overall Grade: C

Greenville's industrial base is healthy and growing, something that very
few metros can say. The manufacturing sector, which accounts for 30 percent
of all local employment, added 2,200 jobs between 1985 and 1990. That's
a major reason why Greenville received a solid B on the job opportunities
test. The local economy's biggest flaw is its stinginess with business opportunities for women and minorities.

34. (tie) Harrisburg

Population: 587,986
Overall Grade: C

Harrisburg's unemployment rate usually is one or two percentage points
lower than the national rate, and the state government deserves much of
the credit. State capitals such as Harrisburg usually have an extra measure
of economic stability. The government sector no longer is expanding, but
it still directly accounts for 22 percent of all jobs in the area. Harrisburg's
property taxes are the second-lowest in the East.

36. Dallas

Population: 3,885,415
Overall Grade: C

The long-running television drama of the same name depicted a Dallas
of unbounded prosperity and unlimited economic power. The reality is
less compelling. Dallas struggled during the energy bust of the 1980s. It
is regaining momentum, but remains behind most Sunbelt metros in terms
of economic opportunities. Explosive growth will continue in Collin and
Denton counties, north of the cities of Dallas and Fort Worth.

37. Columbus

Population: 1,377,419
Overall Grade: C

Most Ohio metros rise and fall as heavy industry rises and falls. Columbus is different, which is why it is in better shape for the future. Manufacturing accounts for only 14 percent of the jobs in Columbus, compared to 22 percent in Cleveland and 20 percent in Toledo. Employment stability and good salaries are found at two of the area's leading employers, the state government and Ohio State University.

38. Omaha

Population: 618,262
Overall Grade: C

Which area will be the growth center of the Midwest: Minneapolis? Kansas City? Indianapolis? The correct (if unlikely) answer is Omaha, with a projected population increase of 22 percent between 1990 and 2020, the highest figure of any Midwestern metro. It's a sharp turnaround from the slow 1980s, the decade that saddled Omaha with a grade of D– on the economic momentum test. Sarpy County, south of the city, has the strongest growth potential in the Omaha area.

39. (tie) Baltimore

Population: 2,382,172
Overall Grade: C

The rebirth of Baltimore's Inner Harbor has received widespread publicity, but it is the suburbs that hold the key to the area's economic future. Several outlying counties have above-average growth potential. Chief among them is Howard County, one of the fastest-growing commuter counties in America, shoehorned between Baltimore and nearby Washington. The population of the entire Baltimore area is expected to increase 18 percent by 2020.

39. (tie) Birmingham

Population: 907,810
Overall Grade: C

Birmingham pulled straight C's on four of the six tests, but the other two provide a study in extremes. The lowest property taxes in the country earned Birmingham the top grade for real estate opportunities. That stands in

sharp contrast to the equality of opportunities test, where Birmingham **113**
finished next to last in the nation. The area's strongest growth will occur
in Shelby County, southeast of the city.

41. Memphis

Population: 981,747
Overall Grade: C

Memphis added nearly 10,000 manufacturing jobs between 1985 and 1990,
a notable exception to the industrial decline of modern America. The area
made its mark, however, in the service sector; it is the home of Federal
Express and the birthplace of the Holiday Inn chain. Memphis has reasonably
priced real estate and is expected to grow fairly rapidly. But there is a
glaringly apparent flaw in Memphis' economy: a grade of F in the equality
of opportunities test.

42. Albany

Population: 874,304
Overall Grade: C

The massive bureaucracy of the New York state government historically
has been a dependable source of jobs for the Albany area, but budget
shortfalls have forced the state to lay off workers in recent years. The
service sector actually took over as Albany's leading employer in the late
1980s. The government's problems had surprisingly little impact on the
local unemployment rate, which remained below the national average. Future
growth is likely to be focused north of the city in Saratoga County.

43. Saint Louis

Population: 2,444,099
Overall Grade: C

Saint Louis once was among America's biggest cities, as well as a primary
jumping-off point for settlers heading west. The 630-foot-high Gateway Arch
towering above the Mississippi River is a tribute to that prosperous past;
it also reminds us that westward expansion eventually dwarfed areas such
as this. Saint Louis' population increased by less than 3 percent during
the 1980s, and future gains are likely to be modest. The exception is Saint
Charles County, west of the city, which has the strongest growth potential
of any county in the Midwest.

44. Grand Rapids

Population: 688,399
Overall Grade: C

Grand Rapids once called itself the furniture capital of the world, but most of the furniture companies headed south long ago. They have been replaced by a diversified mix of high-tech and service industries that has helped Grand Rapids avoid the high unemployment rates found in many Midwestern metros. Ottawa County, which hugs the Lake Michigan shoreline west of the city, has the strongest growth potential in the area.

45. Salt Lake City

Population: 1,072,227
Overall Grade: C

You might say that Salt Lake City's most powerful employer is locally owned and operated. The city is the world headquarters of the Mormon church, which exerts a strong influence on the area's development strategies and politics. But outsiders who expect a narrow-minded religious community are wrong. Salt Lake City received a straight B on the equality of opportunities test. The rest of the story is a mixture of good and bad news: Unemployment generally is low, but the area's retail sector is the weakest in the country.

46. Hartford

Population: 1,123,678
Overall Grade: C

The finance, insurance, and real estate sector is a minor component of most metropolitan economies, but it accounts for an astounding 16 percent of all jobs in Hartford, the insurance capital of the country. The high number of white-collar jobs has a positive impact on the local standard of living. The problem is that Hartford suffers from the New England disease, an overheated real estate market. Only nine of the country's major metro areas have housing that is more expensive than Hartford's.

47. Allentown

Population: 686,688
Overall Grade: C

Allentown was the subject of Billy Joel's 1982 song about the desperation of a community that is losing its heavy industry and has no alternative

source of jobs. But the truth is that the area has a diversified economy, **115**
with an unemployment rate that in recent years has been equal to or even
less than the national average. There can be no dispute about Allentown's
overall grade of C, since it received straight C's on all six tests.

48. Springfield

Population: 602,878
Overall Grade: C

Springfield traces its industrial heritage to George Washington, who
established an armory there in 1794 to make firearms for the new country's
army. Manufacturing still accounts for one of every five jobs in the area,
but insurance and health services also are leading fields of employment.
Springfield shared in New England's general prosperity during the 1980s,
but future growth will be tepid. The area's population is projected to increase
only 14 percent by 2020.

49. Charleston

Population: 506,875
Overall Grade: C

The old joke goes that if one more naval installation were squeezed into
Charleston, the whole area would sink into the Atlantic Ocean. The age
of military cutbacks has saved Charlestonians from such a fate, but the
federal government remains the area's best source of well-paying jobs.
Development is concentrated these days in the outlying counties of Berkeley
and Dorchester.

50. Fresno

Population: 667,490
Overall Grade: C

Fresno, one of the nation's leading agribusiness centers, also has an impressive
record as a population magnet. The Fresno area grew by 30 percent during
the 1980s, and a further increase of 20 percent is expected by 2020. But
the key question is how many of these new residents will find jobs. Fresno's
unemployment rate historically is much higher than the national average.

51. Boston

Population: 3,783,817
Overall Grade: C

Boston was among the nation's hot spots in the mid-1980s, the showpiece of Michael Dukakis'"Massachusetts Miracle." The local economy has cooled considerably since then, burdened by an overheated real estate market and a substantial jump in unemployment. Overcrowding is another problem; only New York City has a higher population density. But not all of the news is bad. Business opportunities in Boston's retail and service sectors are better than in most other places.

52. (tie) Cincinnati

Population: 1,744,124
Overall Grade: C–

What is Ohio's busiest port? The Great Lakes cities of Cleveland and Toledo cannot match the tonnage that slips down the Ohio River from Cincinnati. This surprising fact highlights an economic diversity that is unmatched by many Midwestern metros. But Cincinnati has not escaped one problem found throughout the Midwest: Its rate of future growth is expected to be a sedate 12 percent between 1990 and 2020.

52. (tie) Norfolk

Population: 1,396,107
Overall Grade: C–

The sudden end of the Cold War left a slight air of uncertainty hanging over Norfolk, only natural in an area that is economically dependent on naval installations and shipbuilders. But the unemployment rate remains below the national level, thanks to an active port and a strong tourism industry. Norfolk is the prominent city in the area, but it no longer is the largest. Virginia Beach ranks No. 1 in population in the entire state.

52. (tie) San Antonio

Population: 1,302,099
Overall Grade: C–

San Antonio is another area that has benefited from the presence of large military installations—army and air force, in this case—but now has concerns about future troop levels. The bases are part of the government sector, which is responsible for 23 percent of all area employment. Real estate is affordable in San Antonio, but other indicators are not promising. The unemployment rate typically is higher than the national average, and both the retail and service sectors are weak.

55. Philadelphia

Population: 5,899,345
Overall Grade: C−

Philadelphia, one of America's oldest cities, offers a textbook example of classic metropolitan growth patterns. Philadelphia County and adjacent Delaware County will continue to lose population throughout the 1990s. Expansion will be focused in outlying parts of three suburban counties: Chester in Pennsylvania, Burlington and Gloucester in New Jersey. The Philadelphia area scored in the C range on five of six tests; its worst grade was a D for future growth.

56. Syracuse

Population: 659,864
Overall Grade: C−

Syracuse still proudly calls itself the Salt City, recalling when the area's salt deposits served the nation. But the local economy has long since diversified. Syracuse makes auto parts, steel, chemicals, ball bearings, and electronic components, all the things you would expect a Northern industrial city to make. Unemployment usually is lower than the national average, but the business community does not accept newcomers enthusiastically. Syracuse received a grade of D+ on the equality of opportunities test.

57. New Haven

Population: 804,219
Overall Grade: C−

New Haven is best known as the home of Yale University, but it also is one of New England's industrial centers. The manufacturing sector has cooled in recent years, but still accounts for 17 percent of all local jobs. There are two restraints on economic progress in New Haven. The area has little room to grow; only four metros have higher population densities. And housing is expensive, earning New Haven an F on the real estate opportunities test.

58. Toledo

Population: 614,128
Overall Grade: C–

Toledo's economic health is tied to the fortunes of the domestic auto industry, an unfortunate fact under current conditions. Unemployment has stayed one to two percentage points above the national average in recent years, forcing many residents to look elsewhere for work. Toledo's population fell by 0.4 percent during the 1980s. Demographers predict a modest upswing in coming years, inspired in part by the area's low housing costs.

Below the Norm

59. (tie) Pittsburgh

Population: 2,242,798
Overall Grade: D+

Pittsburgh has undergone an amazing transformation from blue-collar steel city to white-collar service economy. Manufacturing now accounts for only 13 percent of all local jobs. But the metamorphosis was painful, as Pittsburgh lost 7 percent of its population during the 1980s. The high unemployment rate of the mid-1980s has been brought under control, but Pittsburgh nonetheless received a D on the job opportunities test. The area's strength is its broad array of affordable housing.

59. (tie) Rochester

Population: 1,002,410
Overall Grade: D+

Rochester's large employers are dedicated to duplication. Eastman Kodak manufactures cameras and film, while Xerox makes photocopiers. The presence of these two international giants is the major reason that Rochester has one of the country's strongest manufacturing sectors, as well as a fairly high standard of living. The area's problem is that it is duplicating the growth patterns found in most of the East and Midwest. Its population is expected to increase by less than 6 percent by 2020.

61. Providence

Population: 916,270
Overall Grade: D

Providence is poised to become New England's fastest-growing metro over the next quarter-century. Demographers expect its population to expand by 17.7 percent by 2020. New Haven will be slightly behind at 17.3 percent, with the rest of the region trailing. But the key question is whether Providence will be able to assimilate such growth. It already is one of America's most crowded areas, and it is listed among the nation's ten most expensive real estate markets.

62. Dayton

Population: 951,270
Overall Grade: D

Others might dispute the claims, but Dayton proudly calls itself the birthplace of aviation, the refrigerator, and the cash register. These inventions spawned large local industries that were dependable sources of jobs for decade upon decade. But Dayton was not immune from the manufacturing decline that has hit most Midwestern metros in the past 20 years. Jobs left the area, and growth came to a halt. Dayton's population increased just 1 percent during the 1980s.

63. Bakersfield

Population: 543,477
Overall Grade: D

Bakersfield appears at first glance to be poised for a bright future. Its population expanded 35 percent during the 1980s alone. But jobs and business opportunities are tough to find, as shown by the fact that Bakersfield earned F's on those two tests. Double-digit unemployment rates have been common in recent years. Conditions are especially difficult for women and minorities. Bakersfield received a D on the equality of opportunities test.

64. Houston

Population: 3,711,043
Overall Grade: D

Houston's economy has long been dominated by oil and petrochemical industries, the key to its fantastic growth for much of the century, but also the reason for its screeching halt during the energy bust of the 1980s. Demographers do not expect a return to the days of unchecked expansion. The Houston area is predicted to grow more slowly than the national average between 1990 and 2020. There will be local exceptions to this slowdown. Look for strong population gains in Fort Bend County, which is southwest of the city, and Montgomery County, which is north.

65. Baton Rouge

Population: 528,264
Overall Grade: D

Housing in Baton Rouge is affordable. Only four metros received better scores on the real estate opportunities test. But that, unfortunately, is the extent of the good news. Baton Rouge has virtually no economic momentum. The area's largest employer, the government sector, is not in a hiring mood these days. And all four counties within the Baton Rouge metro area have below-average growth potential.

66. Cleveland

Population: 2,759,823
Overall Grade: D

Cleveland's momentum slipped away during the past quarter-century. It was one of only seven metros to lose population during the 1980s, and it is expected to grow by a modest 9 percent between 1990 and 2020. Manufacturing jobs are slowly slipping away, but the good news is that the service sector has picked up much of the slack. The unemployment rate, which historically ran higher than its national counterpart, has been brought in line in recent years.

67. New York City

Population: 17,953,372
Overall Grade: D–

New York City will remain the nation's largest metro in the next century; it still will be the Big Apple. But it won't grow with its old speed. Demographers predict that the New York City area will expand 13 percent by 2020, compared to the national median of nearly 18 percent. Housing costs are among the highest in the country, and overcrowding is a serious problem. Three New Jersey counties—Hunterdon, Ocean, and Somerset—have the best growth potential in the New York City area.

68. Milwaukee

Population: 1,607,183
Overall Grade: D–

Milwaukee's struggle in the 1970s and 1980s was dramatized by the tribulations of its famous brewing industry. The city's three major breweries —Miller, Schlitz, and Pabst—all were acquired by competitors or conglomerates. Schlitz, long advertised as "the beer that made Milwaukee famous," no longer is brewed in the city. Milwaukee received some national publicity in the early 1990s for a small resurgence in its manufacturing sector. But population growth is expected to remain sluggish, with an increase of only 11 percent between 1990 and 2020.

69. Buffalo

Population: 1,189,288
Overall Grade: D–

Buffalo, which historically relied on heavy industry, is in the midst of a painful transition to a diversified economy. The number of manufacturing jobs shrinks annually, though overall unemployment generally is below the national rate. Perhaps the biggest barrier to progress is the fact that Buffalo's business community is closed to outsiders. No other metro received a lower score on the equality of opportunities test. Buffalo's strength is its affordable real estate. Housing costs are lower than in all Eastern metros but Pittsburgh.

Uphill All the Way

70. Detroit

Population: 4,665,236
Overall Grade: F

Detroit, in many ways, is symbolic of the failure of Northern industrial metros to adapt to changing economic conditions. Detroit corporations once dominated the world auto industry; now they speak of layoffs and downsizing. The local decline in manufacturing triggered high unemployment and a population stagnation. The Detroit area is expected to grow by less than 10 percent between 1990 and 2020. The suburban county with the brightest future is Livingston, far northwest of the city.

71. New Orleans

Population: 1,238,816
Overall Grade: F

New Orleans was staggered by the energy bust of the 1980s and never completely recovered. It actually lost population during the decade, putting it in the same class with old Northern industrial cities such as Buffalo, Cleveland, and Detroit. The subsequent turnaround has been slight. New Orleans is expected to expand by an anemic 8 percent between 1990 and 2020. The jobless rate, grossly inflated in the mid-1980s, has come down to normal levels, but all seven major employment sectors are growing more slowly than the national pace.

72. Chicago

Population: 8,065,633
Overall Grade: F

Chicago is fond of calling itself "the city that works," but there is no denying that the area's economy is not functioning smoothly. Only the service sector is reporting substantial job growth. Chicago's once-vaunted manufacturing sector lost 20,000 jobs in the latter half of the 1980s, a slide that has continued. An exception to the gloomy news is McHenry County, northwest of the city, which is the only county in the Chicago area with above-average growth potential.

73. El Paso

Population: 591,610
Overall Grade: F

It is not easy to make money in El Paso, which has the lowest per capita income among the nation's 73 major metropolitan areas. Gloomy facts and figures can be found at almost every turn: About one-fifth of all El Paso residents are living below the poverty level. No other metro has weaker retail and service sectors. The local unemployment rate usually is three to five percentage points above the national average. But the area has not lost hope. The prospect of a U.S.-Mexico free trade agreement holds open the possibility that El Paso could become an important conduit for increased business activity between the two countries.

Regional Leaders

West Palm Beach is No. 1, but that doesn't make it the only metro that can provide you with exciting economic opportunities.

Perhaps you hate heat and humidity, which means that Florida is not for you. Or you are a lifelong Westerner, and you can't conceive of packing up all of your belongings and moving to West Palm Beach. Or you simply have an irrational dislike of cities with three-word names.

The point is that the final scores in this book are not an end. They are a beginning.

Now it is up to you to study the data and match it with your personal needs. Look carefully at the test results in the previous chapter. Scan the total scores and grades on the preceding pages. Work your way through the report cards in the next chapter. Then put together a comprehensive list of the metro areas that are best for you.

You don't need to pay equal attention to all 73 major metros. Ignore the East if it doesn't interest you. Limit yourself to a single state if you wish. Just remember that you can use the overall scores to pick the best metro in any category you choose. There are hundreds of possibilities. Here are a few: some serious, some offbeat.

Best metro north of the 45th parallel: Seattle
Best metro that includes a state capital: Raleigh
Best metro in Ohio: Columbus
Best metro in a landlocked state: Las Vegas
Best metro located in two or more states: Portland
Best metro on the Canadian border: Buffalo
Best metro on the Mexican border: San Diego
Best metro on the Mississippi River: Minneapolis
Best metro whose name starts with the letter P: Phoenix
Best metro whose name ends in "ville": Knoxville
Best metro whose name ends with the word "City": Kansas City
And so on.

Remember that this book is a tool designed to help you find the best metro area for your future. Take all the time you need. Study all the alternatives. The important thing is to be creative and thorough as you conduct your search. We'll get you started by breaking down the results, region by region.

124 East

The East doesn't have much reason to brag. Washington, with an overall grade of B, is the only Eastern metro to be listed in the national top 20. Some might contend that the region can't take sole credit for even this small measure of distinction, since the Washington area includes a portion of the indisputably Southern state of Virginia.

Eleven Eastern metros have grades in the C range, while the other five received marks between D+ and D–. Buffalo is at the bottom of the regional list, ranking 69th nationally.

Economic opportunities are limited in many Eastern metros by three factors:

1. *Population will grow slowly in coming decades.* The East is the oldest and most densely settled part of the country. It doesn't have the room to expand that is found in the South and West. That's why thirteen of the East's seventeen major metropolitan areas are expected to grow at a rate below the national average between 1990 and 2020.

2. *Job creation is behind the national pace.* Slow population growth logically leads to slow job growth. All but two of the region's metros fell below the national rate of job creation between 1985 and 1990.

3. *Real estate is uncommonly expensive.* Crowded conditions have resulted in housing prices along the Atlantic Seaboard that are far in excess of the national norm. Eastern metros received six of the ten worst scores on the real estate opportunities test.

Don't get the wrong idea. You don't have to exclude the East from your personal calculations. But it will require special care for you to find an area where you can reach your economic potential. Here are some places worthy of your consideration:

Smaller metros. The top half of the regional list includes Scranton, Harrisburg, Albany, Allentown, and Springfield. All have metropolitan populations of less than 875,000.

Pennsylvania. Three of the East's seven best metros are in this state: Scranton (second in the region), Harrisburg (third), and Allentown (seventh).

State capitals. Nothing is certain in this era of budget cutting, but state governments historically have generated jobs and economic stability for capital areas. Harrisburg, Albany, Hartford, and Boston are the state capitals among the nine best metros in the East.

Metro Area	National Rank	Points	Grade
1. Washington	(17)	585	B
2. Scranton	(31)	522	C+
3. Harrisburg	(34)	514	C
4. Baltimore	(39)	502	C
5. Albany	(42)	493	C
6. Hartford	(46)	471	C
7. Allentown	(47)	467	C
8. Springfield	(48)	466	C
9. Boston	(51)	451	C
10. Philadelphia	(55)	436	C–
11. Syracuse	(56)	430	C–
12. New Haven	(57)	429	C–
13. (tie) Pittsburgh	(59)	423	D+
Rochester	(59)	423	D+
15. Providence	(61)	420	D
16. New York City	(67)	381	D–
17. Buffalo	(69)	370	D–

126 South

The list for the South looks much like that for the entire country. West Palm Beach and Orlando hold the top two spots in both rankings. Four other Southern metros join them in the national top ten.

The region's economic strength is dramatized by the fact that three Southern areas belong to the exclusive club of Grade A metros: West Palm Beach with an A+, Orlando and Raleigh with straight A's. The marks for the region's other areas break down into the following ranges: ten B's, eleven C's, two D's, and two F's. El Paso—in line with the Southern pattern of duplicating the national list—is last in both the region and the country as a whole.

The South's top metros have three qualities that make them economically attractive.

1. *Population growth will be rapid.* No area in the country is expected to expand more quickly than West Palm Beach, 45.6 percent between 1990 and 2020. Growth rates for six other Southern metros are projected to be 25 percent or better.

2. *Jobs are more plentiful than in the East or Midwest.* Eight of the top fifteen scores on the job opportunities test were registered by Southern areas. Raleigh has the country's lowest unemployment rate. Orlando is second only to Las Vegas in the speed with which it adds new jobs.

3. *Property taxes are the lowest to be found anywhere.* Homeowners benefit from the South's traditional aversion to taxes. The ten areas with the lowest property taxes in the country are all below the Mason-Dixon line.

There obviously is no shortage of Southern metros that offer above-average economic opportunities, as shown by the fact that thirteen areas received A's or B's. But you might want to narrow your search by concentrating on these categories.

The Southeastern corridor. Most of the region's top metros are in a broad belt that sweeps south from Richmond through Raleigh, Greensboro, Knoxville, Charlotte, and Atlanta before reaching Florida.

Florida. This makes your hunt even easier. Florida has five major metropolitan areas. All five are among the top nine metros in the South.

State capitals. The same rule applies as in the East. Raleigh, Nashville, Atlanta, Richmond, Little Rock, and Austin are capitals that are in the top half of the Southern list.

Metro Area	National Rank	Points	Grade
1. West Palm Beach	(1)	820	A+
2. Orlando	(2)	747	A
3. Raleigh	(4)	692	A
4. Knoxville	(8)	635	B+
5. Tampa	(9)	634	B+
6. Miami	(10)	632	B+
7. Nashville	(11)	624	B+
8. Atlanta	(14)	599	B
9. Jacksonville	(16)	595	B
10. Richmond	(19)	578	B
11. Charlotte	(20)	575	B
12. Greensboro	(21)	565	B
13. Little Rock	(22)	560	B–
14. (tie) Austin	(27)	533	C+
Tulsa	(27)	533	C+
16. Oklahoma City	(30)	523	C+
17. Louisville	(33)	520	C
18. Greenville	(34)	514	C
19. Dallas	(36)	508	C
20. Birmingham	(39)	502	C
21. Memphis	(41)	498	C
22. Charleston	(49)	464	C
23. (tie) Norfolk	(52)	447	C–
San Antonio	(52)	447	C–
25. Houston	(64)	408	D
26. Baton Rouge	(65)	391	D
27. New Orleans	(71)	355	F
28. El Paso	(73)	346	F

128 Midwest

The Midwest once was a land of economic opportunity. Easterners in the 19th century, facing shortages of jobs and land in their home region, frequently started new lives along the Great Lakes or on the Great Plains. But times have changed. Americans on the move these days are more likely to push through to the South or West, and many Midwesterners are among them.

Indianapolis has the best economic prospects in today's Midwest, though it ranks only 22nd nationally with a grade of B-. Eight Midwestern areas are in the C range, while three have D's and two have F's. Detroit and Chicago, the Midwest's largest metros, are at the bottom of the regional list.

Three factors help to explain why Midwestern metros generally do not score well.

1. *Population growth has been slow for more than a decade.* The Midwest includes seven of the fourteen areas that had the smallest growth rates in the country between 1980 and 1990. Toledo, Detroit, and Cleveland actually lost population in the 1980s.

2. *Nor are incomes increasing with any great speed.* Per capita income grew at a below-average pace in ten Midwestern metros during the latter half of the 1980s. Only four areas—Grand Rapids, Detroit, Chicago, and Indianapolis—were above the national norm.

3. *New blood often is not welcomed in business.* It is a truism that business opportunities are severely restricted in areas with little or no economic growth. The old guard hangs on, shutting out newcomers. Eleven of the fourteen Midwestern metros are under the national median for minority business ownership; eight areas also are below average when it comes to women in business.

Good economic opportunities still can be found in the Midwest, if you know where to look. Pay special attention to the following places.

Beyond the Mississippi River. The Kansas City, Minneapolis, Omaha, and Saint Louis areas are included in the top half of the Midwestern list. All are astride or completely west of the Mississippi.

Missouri. There are two major metropolitan areas in this state: Kansas City ranks second in the Midwest, while Saint Louis is sixth.

Medium-sized metros. Not too big, not too small. Indianapolis, Kansas City, Columbus, and Cincinnati—all in the group of Midwestern metros with B's or C's—have populations in the range of 1.2 million to 1.8 million.

Metro Area	National Rank	Points	Grade
1. Indianapolis	(22)	560	B–
2. Kansas City	(26)	543	C+
3. Minneapolis	(29)	527	C+
4. Columbus	(37)	507	C
5. Omaha	(38)	506	C
6. Saint Louis	(43)	489	C
7. Grand Rapids	(44)	488	C
8. Cincinnati	(52)	447	C–
9. Toledo	(58)	426	C–
10. Dayton	(62)	417	D
11. Cleveland	(66)	383	D
12. Milwaukee	(68)	380	D–
13. Detroit	(70)	360	F
14. Chicago	(72)	352	F

130 West

"Turn your face to the great West," Horace Greeley wrote in 1855, "and there build up a home and fortune." His advice still holds true.

No region has a higher proportion of above-average metropolitan areas than the West. It has more Grade A metros than any other part of the country: Las Vegas and Seattle with straight A's, Sacramento and Phoenix both at A–. Six other areas have grades of B or B–, leaving just three with C's and only Bakersfield with a D.

The region's strong economic performance is largely the result of three characteristics shared by most of its metros.

1. *Population is expanding rapidly.* Ten Western areas are expected to grow by more than 25 percent between 1990 and 2020. Some of the projected growth rates are meteoric: Phoenix at 42 percent, Las Vegas at 40, San Diego at 37. The West received seven of the top ten scores on the future growth test.

2. *The number of jobs is increasing quickly.* There were fifteen metros in the country that registered job growth of more than 20 percent between 1985 and 1990. Seven were in the West.

3. *The region leads the nation in accepting diversity.* The West made virtually a clean sweep of the top scores in the equality of opportunities test, taking five of the seven A's. Denver has the country's best record of welcoming women into business; Honolulu is the best with minorities.

You can't go too far wrong in the West, given that ten of its fourteen major metropolitan areas have overall grades in the A or B ranges. Strong metros can be found in all parts of the region.

The interior. It is taken as an article of faith that the best economic opportunities in the West are in the coastal states. That is not necessarily true, as shown by the fact that Las Vegas, Phoenix, Denver, and Tucson received high scores.

California. Yes, real estate is expensive, and yes, the big metros are crowded. But there still are places in California where you can do well: Sacramento with an A– and San Diego and San Francisco with straight B's.

The Pacific Northwest. This section considers itself the antithesis of California, but its growth patterns are similar. Seattle and Portland both are in the top half of the Western list.

Metro Area	National Rank	Points	Grade
1. Las Vegas	(3)	730	A
2. Seattle	(5)	677	A
3. Sacramento	(6)	655	A–
4. Phoenix	(7)	638	A–
5. Denver	(12)	614	B
6. San Diego	(13)	603	B
7. Portland	(15)	597	B
8. San Francisco	(18)	584	B
9. (tie) Honolulu	(24)	558	B–
Tucson	(24)	558	B–
11. Los Angeles	(31)	522	C+
12. Salt Lake City	(45)	484	C
13. Fresno	(50)	462	C
14. Bakersfield	(63)	410	D

3

The Report Cards

Welcome to Arlington, Montana, one of the boom cities of the new West. Arlington, which sprawls across the rolling plains of eastern Montana, is the commercial center for a regional economy that is heavily dependent on ranching, wheat farming, and energy industries.

The city of Arlington has 143,362 residents. Its two large suburbs, Lexington and Charlevoix, are in adjacent Rockbridge and Glass counties. The metro area stretches farther east to Rockingham County and south over the state line into Wyoming. The total metro population is 814,417, which means Arlington is roughly the size of Honolulu or New Haven.

There's only one catch to this story. You have probably never heard of Arlington, Montana, nor can you find it in your road atlas. That's because Arlington doesn't exist, except as a fictional example to explain how to use the charts on the following pages.

The rest of this book contains detailed report cards for each of the country's 73 major metropolitan areas, listed in alphabetical order (Arlington not included, of course). You can use these charts to learn much more

134 about the strengths and weaknesses of the metros that have piqued your interest. You will discover the counties with the best growth potential, the cities that have houses in your price range, and the types of jobs that are commonly found in a given metro area.

The package for each area consists of five charts. All statistics are the latest available as of April 1, 1992.

1. *Metro Area Report Card.* This is a summary of information that can be found elsewhere in this book. Included is the area's final score, overall grade, and national and regional ranks, as well as its scores and grades on each of the six tests.

2. *Growth Potential of Metro Area Counties.* This chart provides basic information about all the counties that make up a specific metro area. It also ranks them according to their potential for population growth and economic expansion during the 1990s.

3. *Biggest Cities.* This chart lists the populations of the largest cities in the metro area, as well as the median house prices in each city.

4. *Annual Unemployment Rates.* This is a brief statistical history of recent employment trends. Each year's jobless rate for the metro area is compared to the national rate.

5. *Major Employment Sectors.* This list includes information on seven major job classifications. It reports the number of jobs, the average annual pay, and the recent rate of hiring in each sector within the metro area.

These charts are easy to read—in most cases, self-explanatory—so feel free to turn to them right now. You will find them to be useful tools that will help pinpoint the metro area that is best for you.

But if you run into something that is confusing, or if you just want a thorough briefing before you start, the following information is what you're looking for. Come along for a quick and simple chart-by-chart trip to the Great Plains paradise of Arlington, Montana.

1.

ARLINGTON

Total Points: 542
Overall Grade: C+
National Rank: 27 of 73
Regional Rank: 11 of 14 (West)

Metro Area Report Card   **135**

Category	Points	Grade
Economic Momentum	42	C
Future Growth	65	B
Job Opportunities	33	D
Business Opportunities	51	C+
Real Estate Opportunities	79	B
Equality of Opportunities	52	B
Overall	542	C+

Area Name. The federal government prefers complicated names for metro areas; we don't. The government probably would call this the Arlington-Lexington-Charlevoix Metropolitan Statistical Area, while we just call it the Arlington area.

Each metro in this book is named after its dominant city, which usually is its largest city. (But not always. Norfolk and San Francisco have given their names to metro areas, even though those cities have been surpassed in population by Virginia Beach and San Jose, respectively.)

Total Points. Arlington's total score was 542 points. That translates to an overall grade of C+.

Ranks. Arlington's score was good enough for 27th place among the nation's 73 major metropolitan areas. It finished 11th among the fourteen metros in the West.

Category. The names of the six tests are listed in the category column.

Points. Point totals for the six tests can be found in this column, followed at the bottom by the total score. Arlington's best test score was 79 points for real estate opportunities; its worst was 33 points for job opportunities.

Grade. This column contains Arlington's grades on the six tests, followed by its overall grade. The area's best grade was B, received on three tests. Its worst was a D for job opportunities.

136

2.

Growth Potential of Metro Area Counties

Rank	County	Population	Per Capita Income	Growth Potential Points	Growth Potential Grade
1.	Glass	256,654	$16,742	63	A
2.	Lake, Wyo.	113,946	$17,842	58	B+
3.	Monroe, Wyo.*	74,390	$15,970	43	C+
	Rockbridge*	127,954	$14,967	43	C+
5.	Arlington†	143,362	$13,912	33	C
6.	Rockingham	98,111	$12,327	21	D–

* Tied in rank.
† Independent city.
Counties are in Montana unless otherwise indicated.

Rank. Counties are ranked in order of their growth potential (a concept explained below). The number in this column is the ranking within the metro area itself. Glass County has the strongest growth potential in the Arlington area, while Rockingham County ranks sixth and last.

County. This column includes all counties that make up the metropolitan area, as defined by the federal government. The Arlington area consists of five counties and an independent city.

County Location. State abbreviations follow the names of all counties that are in different states from the metro center. Arlington is in Montana, but Lake and Monroe counties are in Wyoming. A note at the bottom of the chart reminds you of the distinction.

Population. County population figures are from the 1990 census. Glass County, with 256,654 residents, is the most populous county in the Arlington metro.

Per Capita Income. Per capita income statistics are for 1989, as estimated by the U.S. Bureau of Economic Analysis. The most prosperous county in the Arlington metro is Lake County, with annual income of $17,842 per person.

Per capita income is determined by taking the total earnings of all residents and dividing that figure by the county's population (including children). If you want to know the average income for a household of **137** your size, multiply the per capita income figure by your number of family members. The typical family of four in Lake County earns $71,368.

Growth Potential. All other scores and grades in this book are given to metro areas *as a whole,* but growth potential is a measure of the future prospects of *each county* within a metro area. Growth potential is rated on a 100-point scale, using a formula that factors in recent population growth, income growth, and population density.

Glass County, with a score of 63 and a grade of A, will be the likely center for additional growth in the Arlington area, but Rockingham County (21, D–) won't see much activity. Growth potential scores and grades are computed on the same scale for all areas, meaning that you can make direct comparisons of counties in different metros.

Don't be confused. Growth potential is *not* the same thing as economic momentum or future growth, two tests given to metro areas. Growth potential is based on statistics used in both of those tests, making it a hybrid of the two. Consider it a quick measure of growth patterns within a metro.

Asterisks. The asterisks indicate that Monroe and Rockbridge counties, which have identical growth potential scores, are tied for third place.

Daggers. The dagger symbol indicates that Arlington is an independent city that is not part of any county, but legally is considered the equivalent of a county. Independent cities, in real life, are found in four states: Maryland, Missouri, Nevada, and Virginia.

138

3.

Biggest Cities

City	County	Median House Price	Population
Arlington	(independent city)	$98,700	143,362
Lexington	Rockbridge	$112,900	67,877
Charlevoix	Glass	$103,400	54,294
Kohler, Wyo.	Lake	$86,500	27,973
Cedarburg*	Glass	$79,800	24,764
Benton, Wyo.*	Lake	$54,300	22,911
Niawanda, Wyo.	Lake	$70,000	21,246
Madison	Rockingham	$42,300	20,778
Wolverton*	Rockingham	$39,700	20,085

* Census Designated Places. All others are incorporated communities.
Cities are in Montana unless otherwise indicated.

City. This chart identifies the biggest cities in the metropolitan area. They are ranked in order of population, beginning with Arlington, Lexington, and Charlevoix.

County. This column matches each city with the county in which it is located. Lexington is in Rockbridge County, while Cedarburg is in Glass County.

Median House Price. This column tells you how much it would cost to buy a typical house in each city. All figures are from the 1990 census. The median value of a single-family house in Lexington is $112,900, compared to $39,700 in Wolverton. Keep in mind that these values are for 1990 and should be adjusted for subsequent inflation.

Population. Figures are from the 1990 census.

Independent City. Arlington, as an independent city, is not part of any county.

State Abbreviations. These follow the names of all cities that are in different states from the metro center. Arlington is in Montana, but Kohler, Benton, and Niawanda are in Wyoming. A note at the bottom of the chart reminds you of the distinction.

Asterisks. These indicate that Cedarburg, Benton, and Wolverton technically are not cities. Each is a *Census Designated Place,* the name given by the U.S. Census Bureau to unincorporated areas that have all of the other characteristics of cities. These Census Designated Places have substantial populations, thriving malls and business districts, and are considered by local residents to be the same as cities.

Towns and townships in New England, New York, and parts of the Midwest are among the unincorporated areas to be given Census Designated Place status. (Be aware that the government sometimes will select only part of a town to be a Census Designated Place. That explains why town populations can differ from the Census Designated Place populations included in this book.)

Number of Cities. This chart can list as many as ten cities, provided that all ten have 20,000 or more residents. The chart for the Arlington metro has nine cities, the only nine that top the population threshold in that area. There is one exception to this rule. At least three cities will be listed for each metro area, even if some of those cities have fewer than 20,000 residents.

4.

Annual Unemployment Rates

Year	Metro Area	National
1985	8.4%	7.2%
1986	7.9%	7.0%
1987	6.5%	6.2%
1988	5.7%	5.5%
1989	4.8%	5.3%
1990	4.1%	5.5%

Year. The U.S. Bureau of Labor Statistics calculates annual unemployment rates for metropolitan areas. This chart has figures for 1985 through 1990.

Metro Area. The unemployment rate in the Arlington metro declined steadily during the latter half of the 1980s. It was 8.4 percent in 1985, dropping to 4.1 percent by 1990.

140   **National.** The national jobless rate is included for comparison purposes. Unemployment in the United States was 6.2 percent in 1987, the same year that it was 6.5 percent in the Arlington area.

5.

Major Employment Sectors

Sector	Jobs	Market Share	Average Pay	5-Year Trend
Services	83,800	27%	$19,620	Hot
Wholesale and retail trade	77,800	25%	$12,745	Warm
Government	66,900	21%	$23,763	Hot
Manufacturing	44,200	14%	$32,453	Cold
Construction	14,700	5%	$18,950	Cool
Finance, insurance, and real estate	11,300	4%	$22,378	Cold
Transportation and utilities	8,600	3%	n.a.	Warm

Sector. The U.S. Bureau of Labor Statistics divides all non-agricultural jobs into eight employment classifications. This chart includes seven of those sectors. The exception is mining, which is not found in most major metropolitan areas.

Jobs. This column lists the number of jobs in each sector in 1990. There are 66,900 government jobs and 44,200 manufacturing jobs in the Arlington area.

Market Share. The distribution of non-agricultural jobs within the labor market is expressed in percentages. The service sector accounts for 27 percent of all non-farm jobs in the Arlington area, while construction is responsible for 5 percent. The percentages for the seven sectors might not add to 100 percent because of rounding and because mining and unclassified jobs are not included in the chart.

Average Pay. The U.S. Bureau of Labor Statistics estimates the average annual pay for all jobs within each sector. Keep in mind that these figures are for 1989 and should be adjusted for subsequent inflation.

The typical service worker in the Arlington area made $19,620 a year in 1989. You can compare average pay for the same sectors in different metros to get an idea of variations in salary levels (which also gives you an idea of differences in the cost of living). Average pay statistics are **141** unavailable for the transportation and utilities sector.

Five-Year Trend. Employment trends between 1985 and 1990 are summarized by four terms: hot, warm, cool, or cold. The government sector in the Arlington area is expanding rapidly, which means that it is hot. The number of manufacturing jobs in Arlington is declining, the sign of a cold sector.

Each term compares the local and national rates of job growth within an employment sector:

Hot means that the number of local jobs increased more than 5 percentage points faster than the national rate for the same sector between 1985 and 1990.

Warm indicates that local job growth was between 0 and 5 percentage points higher than the national average.

Cool means that the local rate was between 0 and 5 percentage points lower than the national rate.

Cold indicates that the local sector lagged behind the national average by 5 percentage points or more.

There usually is a close correlation between the employment trends column and a metro area's score on the job opportunities test. Consider Las Vegas, which received an A on the test. All seven of its sectors are rated hot.

But keep in mind that the column and the test are measuring two different things. The employment trends column is a narrow indicator; it reflects job growth in a specific sector. The test is a much broader measure; it is based on job growth in all sectors, as well as recent unemployment rates.

That explains a seemingly contradictory case such as Fresno, where six of the seven employment sectors are hot, but the area was given an F on the job opportunities test. The sectors *are* hot. A rapid increase in population during the 1980s triggered a large expansion of Fresno's job base. But even such a frenzied rate of job growth wasn't enough to solve one of the area's worst problems. Fresno's unemployment rate remained the highest among the nation's 73 major metropolitan areas.

ALBANY

Total Points: 493
Overall Grade: C
National Rank: 42 of 73
Regional Rank: 5 of 17 (East)

Metro Area Report Card

Category	Points	Grade
Economic Momentum	51	C+
Future Growth	50	C
Job Opportunities	60	B–
Business Opportunities	52	C+
Real Estate Opportunities	57	C
Equality of Opportunities	25	C
Overall	493	C

Growth Potential of Metro Area Counties

Rank	County	Population	Per Capita Income	Growth Potential Points	Grade
1.	Saratoga	181,276	$18,050	49	B
2.	Albany	292,594	$20,897	41	C
3.	Greene*	44,739	$15,755	38	C
	Rensselaer*	154,429	$17,239	38	C
5.	Schenectady	149,285	$19,435	35	C
6.	Montgomery	51,981	$15,250	29	D+

*Tied in rank.
Entire metro area is in New York.

Biggest Cities

City	County	Median House Price	Population
Albany	Albany	$101,800	101,082
Schenectady	Schenectady	$82,100	65,566
Troy	Rensselaer	$84,400	54,269
Saratoga Springs	Saratoga	$108,800	25,001
Rotterdam*	Schenectady	$89,100	21,228
Amsterdam	Montgomery	$71,000	20,714

*Census Designated Place. All others are incorporated communities.

Annual Unemployment Rates

Year	Metro Area	National
1985	5.2%	7.2%
1986	5.2%	7.0%
1987	4.0%	6.2%
1988	3.6%	5.5%
1989	4.2%	5.3%
1990	3.6%	5.5%

Major Employment Sectors

Sector	Jobs	Market Share	Average Pay	5-Year Trend
Services	118,200	27%	$19,744	Hot
Government	115,700	27%	$27,128	Cool
Wholesale and retail trade	92,600	21%	$12,202	Hot
Manufacturing	46,200	11%	$30,590	Cold
Finance, insurance, and real estate	25,200	6%	$23,285	Hot
Construction	19,500	4%	$26,412	Hot
Transportation and utilities	17,200	4%	n.a.	Cool

ALLENTOWN

Total Points: 467
Overall Grade: C
National Rank: 47 of 73
Regional Rank: 7 of 17 (East)

Metro Area Report Card

Category	Points	Grade
Economic Momentum	46	C
Future Growth	54	C
Job Opportunities	45	C
Business Opportunities	46	C
Real Estate Opportunities	64	C
Equality of Opportunities	23	C
Overall	467	C

Growth Potential of Metro Area Counties

Rank	County	Population	Per Capita Income	Growth Potential Points	Grade
1.	Warren, N.J.	91,607	$21,327	48	B
2.	Northampton	247,105	$17,500	38	C
3.	Lehigh	291,130	$18,822	37	C
4.	Carbon	56,846	$14,284	30	C–

Counties are in Pennsylvania unless otherwise indicated.

Biggest Cities

City	County	Median House Price	Population
Allentown	Lehigh	$76,600	105,090
Bethlehem	Northampton	$90,600	71,428
Easton	Northampton	$80,500	26,276

Annual Unemployment Rates

Year	Metro Area	National
1985	8.0%	7.2%
1986	7.4%	7.0%
1987	5.0%	6.2%
1988	4.4%	5.5%
1989	4.4%	5.3%
1990	5.5%	5.5%

Major Employment Sectors

Sector	Jobs	Market Share	Average Pay	5-Year Trend
Services	75,400	26%	$19,013	Hot
Manufacturing	74,400	26%	$28,130	Cold
Wholesale and retail trade	63,700	22%	$12,240	Hot
Government	31,400	11%	$22,357	Cool
Transportation and utilities	14,700	5%	n.a.	Cool
Finance, insurance, and real estate	14,600	5%	$23,247	Hot
Construction	13,000	5%	$25,389	Hot

ATLANTA

Total Points: 599
Overall Grade: B
National Rank: 14 of 73
Regional Rank: 8 of 28 (South)

Metro Area Report Card

Category	Points	Grade
Economic Momentum	61	B
Future Growth	64	B–
Job Opportunities	60	B–
Business Opportunities	61	B
Real Estate Opportunities	68	C
Equality of Opportunities	40	B–
Overall	599	B

Growth Potential of Metro Area Counties

Rank	County	Population	Per Capita Income	Growth Potential Points	Grade
1.	Fayette	62,415	$21,789	89	A+
2.	Gwinnett	352,910	$18,692	81	A+
3.	Cherokee	90,204	$15,903	77	A
4.	Forsyth*	44,083	$17,601	71	A
	Henry*	58,741	$16,479	71	A
	Paulding*	41,611	$13,802	71	A
	Rockdale	54,091	$17,388	69	A
8.	Cobb	447,745	$20,781	60	A–
9.	Douglas	71,120	$15,094	59	B+
10.	Barrow	29,721	$14,214	56	B+
11.	Coweta	53,853	$14,929	53	B

Growth Potential of Metro Area Counties (continued)

Rank	County	Population	Per Capita Income	Growth Potential Points	Growth Potential Grade
12.	Walton	38,586	$13,376	50	B
13.	Newton	41,808	$13,861	45	B–
14.	Clayton*	182,052	$15,953	43	C+
	Spalding*	54,457	$13,457	43	C+
16.	Fulton	648,951	$21,557	42	C+
17.	Butts	15,326	$12,099	35	C
18.	DeKalb	545,837	$19,860	32	C–

*Tied in rank.
Entire metro area is in Georgia.

Biggest Cities

City	County	Median House Price	Population
Atlanta	Fulton	$71,200	394,017
Sandy Springs*	Fulton	$231,700	67,842
Roswell	Fulton	$142,000	47,923
Marietta	Cobb	$87,500	44,129
East Point	Fulton	$64,500	34,402
Smyrna	Cobb	$78,100	30,981
Candler-McAfee*	DeKalb	$61,600	29,491
North Atlanta*	DeKalb	$98,500	27,812
Dunwoody*	DeKalb	$174,200	26,302
Tucker*	DeKalb	$111,300	25,781

*Census Designated Places. All others are incorporated communities.

Annual Unemployment Rates

Year	Metro Area	National
1985	5.0%	7.2%
1986	4.6%	7.0%
1987	4.7%	6.2%
1988	5.1%	5.5%
1989	5.1%	5.3%
1990	5.1%	5.5%

Major Employment Sectors

Sector	Jobs	Market Share	Average Pay	5-Year Trend
Wholesale and retail trade	404,200	27%	$13,403	Warm
Services	376,400	25%	$22,555	Hot
Government	222,600	15%	$23,648	Hot
Manufacturing	173,600	12%	$27,288	Cold
Transportation and utilities	128,700	9%	n.a.	Hot
Finance, insurance, and real estate	107,900	7%	$30,360	Hot
Construction	67,900	5%	$23,307	Cold

AUSTIN

Total Points: 533
Overall Grade: C+
National Rank: 27 of 73
Regional Rank: 14 of 28 (South)

Metro Area Report Card

Category	Points	Grade
Economic Momentum	43	C
Future Growth	61	C+
Job Opportunities	42	C–
Business Opportunities	53	C+
Real Estate Opportunities	54	C–
Equality of Opportunities	64	B+
Overall	533	C+

Growth Potential of Metro Area Counties

Rank	County	Population	Per Capita Income	Growth Potential Points	Growth Potential Grade
1.	Williamson	139,551	$13,961	64	A
2.	Travis	576,407	$17,097	53	B
3.	Hays	65,614	$12,174	49	B

Entire metro area is in Texas.

Biggest Cities

City	County	Median House Price	Population
Austin	Travis	$72,600	465,622
Round Rock	Williamson	$69,800	30,923
San Marcos	Hays	$58,200	28,743

Annual Unemployment Rates

Year	Metro Area	National
1985	4.2%	7.2%
1986	5.6%	7.0%
1987	6.5%	6.2%
1988	6.1%	5.5%
1989	5.4%	5.3%
1990	4.6%	5.5%

Major Employment Sectors

Sector	Jobs	Market Share	Average Pay	5-Year Trend
Government	107,400	28%	$22,062	Warm
Services	96,300	26%	$20,058	Warm
Wholesale and retail trade	77,400	21%	$11,244	Cold
Manufacturing	48,300	13%	$29,619	Hot
Finance, insurance, and real estate	23,500	6%	$22,919	Cold
Construction	11,900	3%	$21,278	Cold
Transportation and utilities	11,700	3%	n.a.	Warm

BAKERSFIELD

Total Points: 410
Overall Grade: D
National Rank: 63 of 73
Regional Rank: 14 of 14 (West)

Metro Area Report Card

Category	Points	Grade
Economic Momentum	52	C+
Future Growth	79	A–
Job Opportunities	18	F
Business Opportunities	7	F
Real Estate Opportunities	53	C–
Equality of Opportunities	14	D
Overall	410	D

Growth Potential of Metro Area County

County	Population	Per Capita Income	Growth Potential Points	Grade
Kern	543,477	$14,856	37	C

Entire metro area is in California.

Biggest Cities

City	County	Median House Price	Population
Bakersfield	Kern	$91,200	174,820
Ridgecrest	Kern	$87,700	27,725
Oildale*	Kern	$67,900	26,553
Delano	Kern	$65,400	22,762

*Census Designated Place. All others are incorporated communities.

Annual Unemployment Rates

Year	Metro Area	National
1985	11.5%	7.2%
1986	12.0%	7.0%
1987	10.5%	6.2%
1988	10.2%	5.5%
1989	10.3%	5.3%
1990	10.5%	5.5%

Major Employment Sectors

Sector	Jobs	Market Share	Average Pay	5-Year Trend
Government	43,700	25%	$26,561	Hot
Wholesale and retail trade	40,200	23%	$12,404	Cool
Services	36,000	21%	$19,872	Hot
Construction	11,300	7%	$26,033	Hot
Manufacturing	10,900	6%	$28,975	Warm
Transportation and utilities	8,300	5%	n.a.	Cold
Finance, insurance, and real estate	6,800	4%	$22,341	Warm

BALTIMORE

Total Points: 502
Overall Grade: C
National Rank: 39 of 73
Regional Rank: 4 of 17 (East)

Metro Area Report Card

Category	Points	Grade
Economic Momentum	62	B+
Future Growth	41	D+
Job Opportunities	55	C
Business Opportunities	40	C
Real Estate Opportunities	71	C
Equality of Opportunities	28	C
Overall	502	C

Growth Potential of Metro Area Counties

Rank	County	Population	Per Capita Income	Growth Potential Points	Grade
1.	Howard	187,328	$28,252	74	A
2.	Harford	182,132	$20,023	59	B+
3.	Queen Anne's	33,953	$19,897	57	B+
4.	Carroll	123,372	$20,323	56	B+
5.	Anne Arundel	427,239	$21,772	46	B–
6.	Baltimore County	692,134	$21,725	37	C
7.	Baltimore city†	736,014	$16,311	19	F

†Independent city.
Entire metro area is in Maryland.

154   Biggest Cities

City	County	Median House Price	Population
Baltimore	(independent city)	$54,700	736,014
Columbia*	Howard	$150,500	75,883
Dundalk*	Baltimore	$68,400	65,800
Towson*	Baltimore	$134,600	49,445
Ellicott City*	Howard	$192,100	41,396
Essex*	Baltimore	$76,900	40,872
Glen Burnie*	Anne Arundel	$93,400	37,305
Catonsville*	Baltimore	$110,800	35,233
Annapolis	Anne Arundel	$138,500	33,187
Woodlawn*	Baltimore	$95,300	32,907

*Census Designated Places. All others are incorporated communities.

Annual Unemployment Rates

Year	Metro Area	National
1985	5.3%	7.2%
1986	5.2%	7.0%
1987	4.7%	6.2%
1988	4.9%	5.5%
1989	4.0%	5.3%
1990	5.1%	5.5%

Major Employment Sectors

Sector	Jobs	Market Share	Average Pay	5-Year Trend
Services	330,200	29%	$21,024	Hot
Wholesale and retail trade	269,900	23%	$12,696	Warm
Government	218,200	19%	$26,676	Cold
Manufacturing	130,000	11%	$30,709	Cold
Finance, insurance, and real estate	76,100	7%	$28,470	Cool
Construction	75,400	7%	$24,572	Hot
Transportation and utilities	56,400	5%	n.a.	Cold

BATON ROUGE

Total Points: 391
Overall Grade: D
National Rank: 65 of 73
Regional Rank: 26 of 28 (South)

Metro Area Report Card

Category	Points	Grade
Economic Momentum	21	F
Future Growth	41	D+
Job Opportunities	27	F
Business Opportunities	30	D
Real Estate Opportunities	89	A
Equality of Opportunities	22	C
Overall	391	D

Growth Potential of Metro Area Parishes

Rank	Parish	Population	Per Capita Income	Growth Potential Points	Grade
1.	Ascension*	58,214	$12,224	29	D+
	East Baton Rouge*	380,105	$16,236	29	D+
3.	Livingston	70,526	$9,902	28	D
4.	West Baton Rouge	19,419	$11,869	24	D

*Tied in rank.
Entire metro area is in Louisiana.

Biggest Cities

City	Parish	Median House Price	Population
Baton Rouge	East Baton Rouge	$67,900	219,531
Shenandoah*	East Baton Rouge	$99,900	13,429
Baker	East Baton Rouge	$54,500	13,233

*Census Designated Place. All others are incorporated communities.

Annual Unemployment Rates

Year	Metro Area	National
1985	10.3%	7.2%
1986	10.9%	7.0%
1987	10.0%	6.2%
1988	9.3%	5.5%
1989	6.7%	5.3%
1990	5.4%	5.5%

Major Employment Sectors

Sector	Jobs	Market Share	Average Pay	5-Year Trend
Government	54,400	23%	$19,211	Cold
Services	53,600	23%	$18,901	Hot
Wholesale and retail trade	53,300	23%	$10,776	Cold
Construction	27,300	12%	$24,045	Hot
Manufacturing	22,600	10%	$36,057	Hot
Finance, insurance, and real estate	13,000	6%	$21,245	Cold
Transportation and utilities	11,100	5%	n.a.	Warm

BIRMINGHAM

Total Points: 502
Overall Grade: C
National Rank: 39 of 73
Regional Rank: 20 of 28 (South)

Metro Area Report Card

Category	Points	Grade
Economic Momentum	40	C
Future Growth	58	C
Job Opportunities	47	C
Business Opportunities	41	C
Real Estate Opportunities	96	A+
Equality of Opportunities	3	F
Overall	502	C

Growth Potential of Metro Area Counties

Rank	County	Population	Per Capita Income	Growth Potential Points	Growth Potential Grade
1.	Shelby	99,358	$15,743	62	A–
2.	Saint Clair	50,009	$12,050	38	C
3.	Jefferson	651,525	$16,597	34	C
4.	Blount	39,248	$12,292	30	C–
5.	Walker	67,670	$13,172	25	D

Entire metro area is in Alabama.

Biggest Cities

City	County	Median House Price	Population
Birmingham	Jefferson	$44,500	265,968
Hoover	Jefferson	$92,600	39,788
Bessemer	Jefferson	$39,100	33,497
Homewood	Jefferson	$88,600	22,922
Center Point*	Jefferson	$62,900	22,658

*Census Designated Place. All others are incorporated communities.

Annual Unemployment Rates

Year	Metro Area	National
1985	7.2%	7.2%
1986	8.3%	7.0%
1987	6.7%	6.2%
1988	6.0%	5.5%
1989	5.7%	5.3%
1990	5.4%	5.5%

Major Employment Sectors

Sector	Jobs	Market Share	Average Pay	5-Year Trend
Services	105,500	25%	$19,986	Hot
Wholesale and retail trade	99,600	24%	$11,726	Warm
Government	65,400	16%	$21,544	Warm
Manufacturing	57,600	14%	$23,292	Warm
Transportation and utilities	32,600	8%	n.a.	Warm
Finance, insurance, and real estate	30,600	7%	$24,761	Warm
Construction	23,700	6%	$21,990	Warm

BOSTON

Total Points: 451
Overall Grade: C
National Rank: 51 of 73
Regional Rank: 9 of 17 (East)

Metro Area Report Card

Category	Points	Grade
Economic Momentum	58	B
Future Growth	16	F
Job Opportunities	49	C
Business Opportunities	67	A–
Real Estate Opportunities	34	D–
Equality of Opportunities	45	B
Overall	451	C

Growth Potential of Metro Area Counties

Rank	County	Population	Per Capita Income	Growth Potential Points	Grade
1.	Plymouth	435,276	$20,929	50	B
2.	Essex	670,080	$22,793	40	C
3.	Norfolk	616,087	$26,379	38	C
4.	Middlesex	1,398,468	$24,923	37	C
5.	Suffolk	663,906	$21,676	30	C–

Entire metro area is in Massachusetts.

Biggest Cities

City	County	Median House Price	Population
Boston	Suffolk	$161,400	574,283
Lowell	Middlesex	$131,100	103,439
Cambridge	Middlesex	$263,800	95,802
Brockton	Plymouth	$131,700	92,788
Quincy	Norfolk	$161,100	84,985
Newton	Middlesex	$293,400	82,585
Lynn	Essex	$139,200	81,245
Somerville	Middlesex	$165,800	76,210
Lawrence	Essex	$129,600	70,207
Framingham*	Middlesex	$184,700	64,994

*Census Designated Place. All others are incorporated communities.

Annual Unemployment Rates

Year	Metro Area	National
1985	3.4%	7.2%
1986	3.3%	7.0%
1987	2.7%	6.2%
1988	2.8%	5.5%
1989	3.4%	5.3%
1990	5.1%	5.5%

The U.S. Bureau of Labor Statistics calculates the unemployment rate for a geographic area that is slightly different from the Boston metro area defined by this book. Selected towns in the outer portion of the metro area are not included in the above statistics.

Major Employment Sectors

Sector	Jobs	Market Share	Average Pay	5-Year Trend
Services	590,000	35%	$25,670	Cool
Wholesale and retail trade	369,900	22%	$14,586	Cold
Manufacturing	240,100	14%	$33,161	Cold
Government	199,400	12%	$27,682	Cold
Finance, insurance, and real estate	146,200	9%	$33,822	Cool
Transportation and utilities	74,800	4%	n.a.	Cold
Construction	51,300	3%	$31,420	Cold

All figures are for the modified metro area used by the U.S. Bureau of Labor Statistics in its calculations.

BUFFALO

Total Points: 370
Overall Grade: D–
National Rank: 69 of 73
Regional Rank: 17 of 17 (East)

Metro Area Report Card

Category	Points	Grade
Economic Momentum	37	C–
Future Growth	31	D–
Job Opportunities	47	C
Business Opportunities	46	C
Real Estate Opportunities	62	C
Equality of Opportunities	1	F
Overall	370	D–

Growth Potential of Metro Area Counties

Rank	County	Population	Per Capita Income	Growth Potential Points	Grade
1.	Niagara	220,756	$16,183	34	C
2.	Erie	968,532	$17,724	30	C–

Entire metro area is in New York.

Biggest Cities

City	County	Median House Price	Population
Buffalo	Erie	$46,700	328,123
Cheektowaga*	Erie	$69,400	84,387
Tonawanda*	Erie	$74,800	65,284
Niagara Falls	Niagara	$45,100	61,840
West Seneca*	Erie	$78,700	47,866
North Tonawanda	Niagara	$68,100	34,989
Lockport	Niagara	$55,200	24,426
Lackawanna	Erie	$58,200	20,585

*Census Designated Places. All others are incorporated communities.

Annual Unemployment Rates

Year	Metro Area	National
1985	7.3%	7.2%
1986	7.2%	7.0%
1987	5.5%	6.2%
1988	5.0%	5.5%
1989	5.8%	5.3%
1990	4.8%	5.5%

Unemployment statistics for Niagara County were not available from the U.S. Bureau of Labor Statistics. The above figures are for Erie County.

Major Employment Sectors **165**

Sector	Jobs	Market Share	Average Pay	5-Year Trend
Services	145,500	27%	$16,639	Hot
Wholesale and retail trade	136,200	25%	$9,994	Warm
Manufacturing	97,300	18%	$29,765	Cold
Government	89,400	16%	$26,875	Cold
Finance, insurance, and real estate	29,500	5%	$24,326	Hot
Transportation and utilities	27,200	5%	n.a.	Warm
Construction	22,800	4%	$25,098	Hot

The above figures are for the entire metro area, including Niagara County.

CHARLESTON

Total Points: 464
Overall Grade: C
National Rank: 49 of 73
Regional Rank: 22 of 28 (South)

Metro Area Report Card

Category	Points	Grade
Economic Momentum	26	D
Future Growth	65	B
Job Opportunities	69	B
Business Opportunities	35	C–
Real Estate Opportunities	71	C
Equality of Opportunities	13	D
Overall	464	C

Growth Potential of Metro Area Counties

Rank	County	Population	Per Capita Income	Growth Potential Points	Grade
1.	Dorchester	83,060	$12,506	52	B
2.	Berkeley	128,776	$11,244	47	B
3.	Charleston	295,039	$12,775	43	C+

Entire metro area is in South Carolina.

Biggest Cities

City	County	Median House Price	Population
Charleston	Charleston	$86,600	80,414
North Charleston	Charleston	$60,100	70,218
Mount Pleasant	Charleston	$96,900	30,108
Goose Creek	Berkeley	$68,700	24,692
Summerville	Dorchester	$81,000	22,519

Annual Unemployment Rates

Year	Metro Area	National
1985	4.4%	7.2%
1986	4.7%	7.0%
1987	4.6%	6.2%
1988	3.9%	5.5%
1989	4.2%	5.3%
1990	3.4%	5.5%

Major Employment Sectors

Sector	Jobs	Market Share	Average Pay	5-Year Trend
Government	54,600	26%	$24,741	Warm
Wholesale and retail trade	52,000	25%	$10,380	Hot
Services	46,000	22%	$15,344	Hot
Manufacturing	21,400	10%	$25,013	Hot
Construction	16,200	8%	$17,969	Hot
Transportation and utilities	10,900	5%	n.a.	Hot
Finance, insurance, and real estate	7,800	4%	$19,963	Cold

CHARLOTTE

Total Points: 575
Overall Grade: B
National Rank: 20 of 73
Regional Rank: 11 of 28 (South)

Metro Area Report Card

Category	Points	Grade
Economic Momentum	55	B–
Future Growth	57	C
Job Opportunities	73	A–
Business Opportunities	54	B–
Real Estate Opportunities	80	B
Equality of Opportunities	17	C–
Overall	575	B

Growth Potential of Metro Area Counties

Rank	County	Population	Per Capita Income	Growth Potential Points	Growth Potential Grade
1.	Mecklenburg	511,433	$20,040	53	B
2.	Cabarrus	98,935	$15,571	49	B
3.	Lincoln*	50,319	$14,397	48	B
	Union*	84,211	$16,535	48	B
	York, S.C.*	131,497	$15,330	48	B
6.	Gaston	175,093	$15,194	45	B–
7.	Rowan	110,605	$15,011	41	C

*Tied in rank.
Counties are in North Carolina unless otherwise indicated.

Biggest Cities

City	County	Median House Price	Population
Charlotte	Mecklenburg	$81,300	395,934
Gastonia	Gaston	$60,200	54,732
Rock Hill, S.C.	York	$56,300	41,643
Kannapolis	Cabarrus	$46,700	29,696
Concord	Cabarrus	$59,600	27,347
Salisbury	Rowan	$55,500	23,087

Cities are in North Carolina unless otherwise indicated.

Annual Unemployment Rates

Year	Metro Area	National
1985	5.1%	7.2%
1986	4.6%	7.0%
1987	3.8%	6.2%
1988	3.2%	5.5%
1989	3.2%	5.3%
1990	3.5%	5.5%

Major Employment Sectors

Sector	Jobs	Market Share	Average Pay	5-Year Trend
Wholesale and retail trade	154,000	24%	$12,768	Hot
Manufacturing	153,800	24%	$23,088	Warm
Services	124,100	20%	$19,176	Hot
Government	71,300	11%	$21,623	Hot
Transportation and utilities	51,300	8%	n.a.	Hot
Finance, insurance, and real estate	38,200	6%	$27,727	Hot
Construction	37,200	6%	$21,407	Hot

CHICAGO

Total Points: 352
Overall Grade: F
National Rank: 72 of 73
Regional Rank: 14 of 14 (Midwest)

Metro Area Report Card

Category	Points	Grade
Economic Momentum	41	C
Future Growth	23	F
Job Opportunities	41	C–
Business Opportunities	32	D+
Real Estate Opportunities	56	C–
Equality of Opportunities	20	C
Overall	352	F

Growth Potential of Metro Area Counties

Rank	County	Population	Per Capita Income	Growth Potential Points	Grade
1.	McHenry	183,241	$20,742	50	B
2.	Lake, Ill.	516,418	$25,804	42	C+
3.	Kane*	317,471	$19,577	39	C
	Will*	357,313	$17,788	39	C
5.	Kenosha, Wis.	128,181	$17,006	37	C
6.	Porter, Ind.	128,932	$16,618	35	C
7.	Kendall	39,413	$19,670	31	C–
8.	DuPage	781,666	$24,958	29	D+
9.	Grundy	32,337	$17,897	26	D
10.	Lake, Ind.	475,594	$15,017	22	D–
11.	Cook	5,105,067	$19,658	15	F

*Tied in rank.
Counties are in Illinois unless otherwise indicated. State names are listed with both Lake counties to prevent confusion.

Biggest Cities

City	County	Median House Price	Population
Chicago	Cook	$78,700	2,783,726
Gary, Ind.	Lake	$31,700	116,646
Aurora	Kane	$81,900	99,581
Naperville	DuPage	$176,500	85,351
Hammond, Ind.	Lake	$45,500	84,236
Kenosha, Wis.	Kenosha	$58,700	80,352
Elgin	Kane	$96,800	77,010
Joliet	Will	$64,500	76,836
Arlington Heights	Cook	$169,100	75,460
Evanston	Cook	$184,800	73,233

Cities are in Illinois unless otherwise indicated.

Annual Unemployment Rates

Year	Metro Area	National
1985	8.4%	7.2%
1986	7.6%	7.0%
1987	6.8%	6.2%
1988	6.1%	5.5%
1989	5.5%	5.3%
1990	5.8%	5.5%

Major Employment Sectors

Sector	Jobs	Market Share	Average Pay	5-Year Trend
Services	1,066,000	27%	$23,340	Warm
Wholesale and retail trade	951,600	24%	$13,560	Cool
Manufacturing	733,700	19%	$30,597	Cool
Government	481,700	12%	$25,878	Cool
Finance, insurance, and real estate	303,200	8%	$32,953	Cool
Transportation and utilities	244,100	6%	n.a.	Warm
Construction	175,400	4%	$33,306	Hot

CINCINNATI

Total Points: 447
Overall Grade: C–
National Rank: 52 of 73
Regional Rank: 8 of 14 (Midwest)

Metro Area Report Card

Category	Points	Grade
Economic Momentum	38	C
Future Growth	42	C–
Job Opportunities	58	C+
Business Opportunities	35	C–
Real Estate Opportunities	78	B–
Equality of Opportunities	20	C
Overall	447	C–

Growth Potential of Metro Area Counties

Rank	County	Population	Per Capita Income	Growth Potential Points	Grade
1.	Boone, Ky.	57,589	$16,609	49	B
2.	Warren	113,909	$15,639	47	B
3.	Clermont	150,187	$15,023	46	B–
4.	Butler	291,479	$16,029	40	C
5.	Campbell, Ky.	83,866	$15,277	37	C
6.	Dearborn, Ind.*	38,835	$14,458	35	C
	Kenton, Ky.*	142,031	$15,816	35	C
8.	Hamilton	866,228	$19,046	20	F

*Tied in rank.
Counties are in Ohio unless otherwise indicated.

Biggest Cities

City	County	Median House Price	Population
Cincinnati	Hamilton	$61,900	364,040
Hamilton	Butler	$53,700	61,368
Middletown	Butler	$57,600	46,022
Covington, Ky.	Kenton	$41,600	43,264
Fairfield	Butler	$86,300	39,729
Norwood	Hamilton	$51,800	23,674

Cities are in Ohio unless otherwise indicated.

Annual Unemployment Rates

Year	Metro Area	National
1985	7.3%	7.2%
1986	6.5%	7.0%
1987	5.9%	6.2%
1988	5.1%	5.5%
1989	4.5%	5.3%
1990	4.2%	5.5%

Unemployment statistics for Butler County were not available from the U.S. Bureau of Labor Statistics. The above figures are for the remainder of the metro area.

Major Employment Sectors

Sector	Jobs	Market Share	Average Pay	5-Year Trend
Services	193,100	26%	$18,792	Hot
Wholesale and retail trade	189,500	25%	$11,432	Hot
Manufacturing	148,100	20%	$31,998	Cool
Government	94,200	13%	$23,681	Warm
Finance, insurance, and real estate	43,800	6%	$24,764	Hot
Transportation and utilities	41,200	6%	n.a.	Hot
Construction	33,900	5%	$23,664	Hot

Statistics for Butler County were not available from the U.S. Bureau of Labor Statistics. The above figures are for the remainder of the metro area.

CLEVELAND

Total Points: 383
Overall Grade: D
National Rank: 66 of 73
Regional Rank: 11 of 14 (Midwest)

Metro Area Report Card

Category	Points	Grade
Economic Momentum	31	D
Future Growth	29	D–
Job Opportunities	42	C–
Business Opportunities	43	C
Real Estate Opportunities	72	C+
Equality of Opportunities	18	C–
Overall	383	D

Growth Potential of Metro Area Counties

Rank	County	Population	Per Capita Income	Growth Potential Points	Grade
1.	Medina	122,354	$17,773	39	C
2.	Geauga*	81,129	$19,421	36	C
	Portage*	142,585	$15,076	36	C
4.	Lorain	271,126	$15,286	32	C–
5.	Lake	215,499	$18,141	29	D+
6.	Summit	514,990	$17,276	27	D
7.	Cuyahoga	1,412,140	$19,722	14	F

*Tied in rank.
Entire metro area is in Ohio.

Biggest Cities

City	County	Median House Price	Population
Cleveland	Cuyahoga	$40,900	505,616
Akron	Summit	$43,800	223,019
Parma	Cuyahoga	$74,200	87,876
Lorain	Lorain	$52,300	71,245
Lakewood	Cuyahoga	$73,200	59,718
Elyria	Lorain	$56,300	56,746
Euclid	Cuyahoga	$65,000	54,875
Cleveland Heights	Cuyahoga	$71,500	54,052
Cuyahoga Falls	Summit	$61,500	48,950
Mentor	Lake	$89,800	47,358

Annual Unemployment Rates

Year	Metro Area	National
1985	8.4%	7.2%
1986	7.6%	7.0%
1987	6.5%	6.2%
1988	5.6%	5.5%
1989	5.0%	5.3%
1990	4.9%	5.5%

Unemployment statistics for Lorain County were not available from the U.S. Bureau of Labor Statistics. The above figures are for the remainder of the metro area.

Major Employment Sectors

Sector	Jobs	Market Share	Average Pay	5-Year Trend
Services	328,900	27%	$20,427	Hot
Wholesale and retail trade	297,100	24%	$11,250	Warm
Manufacturing	273,600	22%	$31,475	Cool
Government	164,400	13%	$24,037	Cold
Finance, insurance, and real estate	68,800	6%	$25,934	Warm
Transportation and utilities	56,700	5%	n.a.	Cool
Construction	45,200	4%	$27,234	Hot

Statistics for Lorain County were not available from the U.S. Bureau of Labor Statistics. The above figures are for the remainder of the metro area.

COLUMBUS

Total Points: 507
Overall Grade: C
National Rank: 37 of 73
Regional Rank: 4 of 14 (Midwest)

Metro Area Report Card

Category	Points	Grade
Economic Momentum	43	C
Future Growth	55	C
Job Opportunities	60	B–
Business Opportunities	38	C–
Real Estate Opportunities	76	C+
Equality of Opportunities	33	C
Overall	507	C

Growth Potential of Metro Area Counties

Rank	County	Population	Per Capita Income	Growth Potential Points	Grade
1.	Delaware	66,929	$17,664	50	B
2.	Fairfield	103,461	$14,980	39	C
3.	Madison	37,068	$14,764	34	C
4.	Licking*	128,300	$15,417	33	C
	Pickaway*	48,255	$13,393	33	C
	Union*	31,969	$16,655	33	C
7.	Franklin	961,437	$17,917	31	C–

*Tied in rank.
Entire metro area is in Ohio.

Biggest Cities

City	County	Median House Price	Population
Columbus	Franklin	$66,000	632,910
Newark	Licking	$49,500	44,389
Lancaster	Fairfield	$51,700	34,507
Upper Arlington	Franklin	$141,800	34,128
Westerville	Franklin	$109,000	30,269
Gahanna	Franklin	$87,600	27,791
Reynoldsburg	Franklin	$78,700	25,748
Whitehall	Franklin	$57,600	20,572
Delaware	Delaware	$68,100	20,030

Annual Unemployment Rates

Year	Metro Area	National
1985	6.7%	7.2%
1986	6.1%	7.0%
1987	5.4%	6.2%
1988	4.9%	5.5%
1989	4.7%	5.3%
1990	4.4%	5.5%

Major Employment Sectors   **181**

Sector	Jobs	Market Share	Average Pay	5-Year Trend
Wholesale and retail trade	184,100	25%	$12,393	Hot
Services	182,700	25%	$19,506	Hot
Government	129,300	18%	$24,982	Warm
Manufacturing	104,500	14%	$29,284	Cool
Finance, insurance, and real estate	60,700	8%	$25,088	Hot
Transportation and utilities	30,900	4%	n.a.	Hot
Construction	29,500	4%	$24,281	Hot

DALLAS

Total Points: 508
Overall Grade: C
National Rank: 36 of 73
Regional Rank: 19 of 28 (South)

Metro Area Report Card

Category	Points	Grade
Economic Momentum	37	C–
Future Growth	51	C
Job Opportunities	44	C
Business Opportunities	48	C
Real Estate Opportunities	64	C
Equality of Opportunities	62	B+
Overall	508	C

Growth Potential of Metro Area Counties

Rank	County	Population	Per Capita Income	Growth Potential Points	Growth Potential Grade
1.	Collin	264,036	$22,777	82	A+
2.	Denton	273,525	$18,688	79	A
3.	Rockwall	25,604	$16,409	58	B+
4.	Ellis	85,167	$15,055	46	B–
5.	Johnson*	97,165	$14,215	45	B–
	Parker*	64,785	$14,553	45	B–
7.	Tarrant	1,170,103	$17,686	42	C+
8.	Kaufman	52,220	$13,779	35	C
9.	Dallas	1,852,810	$19,602	26	D

*Tied in rank.
Entire metro area is in Texas.

Biggest Cities

City	County	Median House Price	Population
Dallas	Dallas	$78,800	1,006,877
Fort Worth	Tarrant	$59,900	447,619
Arlington	Tarrant	$82,800	261,721
Garland	Dallas	$73,100	180,650
Irving	Dallas	$79,400	155,037
Plano	Collin	$114,100	128,713
Mesquite	Dallas	$68,700	101,484
Grand Prairie	Dallas	$68,600	99,616
Carrollton	Denton	$99,700	82,169
Richardson	Dallas	$110,000	74,840

Annual Unemployment Rates

Year	Metro Area	National
1985	4.8%	7.2%
1986	6.0%	7.0%
1987	6.5%	6.2%
1988	5.9%	5.5%
1989	5.5%	5.3%
1990	5.2%	5.5%

Major Employment Sectors

Sector	Jobs	Market Share	Average Pay	5-Year Trend
Wholesale and retail trade	503,300	26%	$13,923	Cold
Services	501,600	26%	$22,285	Hot
Manufacturing	339,000	17%	$29,259	Cool
Government	234,900	12%	$23,502	Hot
Finance, insurance, and real estate	153,100	8%	$29,080	Cold
Transportation and utilities	137,600	7%	n.a.	Hot
Construction	69,000	4%	$22,837	Cold

DAYTON

Total Points: 417
Overall Grade: D
National Rank: 62 of 73
Regional Rank: 10 of 14 (Midwest)

Metro Area Report Card

Category	Points	Grade
Economic Momentum	32	D+
Future Growth	43	C–
Job Opportunities	47	C
Business Opportunities	30	D
Real Estate Opportunities	80	B
Equality of Opportunities	21	C
Overall	417	D

Growth Potential of Metro Area Counties

Rank	County	Population	Per Capita Income	Growth Potential Points	Growth Potential Grade
1.	Greene	136,731	$16,839	42	C+
2.	Clark	147,548	$15,633	36	C
3.	Miami	93,182	$16,278	35	C
4.	Montgomery	573,809	$17,372	28	D

Entire metro area is in Ohio.

Biggest Cities

City	County	Median House Price	Population
Dayton	Montgomery	$43,200	182,044
Springfield	Clark	$42,000	70,487
Kettering	Montgomery	$77,900	60,569
Huber Heights	Montgomery	$65,900	38,696
Beavercreek	Greene	$97,100	33,626
Fairborn	Greene	$61,800	31,300
Xenia	Greene	$52,900	24,664
Centerville	Montgomery	$111,700	21,082
Piqua	Miami	$46,200	20,612

Annual Unemployment Rates

Year	Metro Area	National
1985	7.2%	7.2%
1986	6.6%	7.0%
1987	5.6%	6.2%
1988	5.2%	5.5%
1989	5.1%	5.3%
1990	5.3%	5.5%

Major Employment Sectors

Sector	Jobs	Market Share	Average Pay	5-Year Trend
Services	118,200	26%	$19,743	Hot
Manufacturing	102,600	23%	$32,031	Cold
Wholesale and retail trade	101,900	23%	$10,680	Warm
Government	77,100	17%	$23,173	Cool
Transportation and utilities	18,400	4%	n.a.	Hot
Finance, insurance, and real estate	17,300	4%	$21,801	Cold
Construction	16,100	4%	$23,781	Hot

DENVER

Total Points: 614
Overall Grade: B
National Rank: 12 of 73
Regional Rank: 5 of 14 (West)

Metro Area Report Card

Category	Points	Grade
Economic Momentum	25	D–
Future Growth	74	B+
Job Opportunities	38	D+
Business Opportunities	76	A
Real Estate Opportunities	60	C
Equality of Opportunities	80	A
Overall	614	B

Growth Potential of Metro Area Counties

Rank	County	Population	Per Capita Income	Growth Potential Points	Grade
1.	Douglas	60,391	$21,972	71	A
2.	Arapahoe	391,511	$20,663	50	B
3.	Boulder	225,339	$20,203	47	B
4.	Jefferson	438,430	$19,891	42	C+
5.	Adams	265,038	$14,306	35	C
6.	Denver	467,610	$20,059	13	F

Entire metro area is in Colorado.

Biggest Cities

City	County	Median House Price	Population
Denver	Denver	$79,000	467,610
Aurora	Arapahoe	$80,200	222,103
Lakewood	Jefferson	$91,400	126,481
Arvada	Jefferson	$89,800	89,235
Boulder	Boulder	$122,700	83,312
Westminster	Adams	$85,700	74,625
Thornton	Adams	$75,600	55,031
Longmont	Boulder	$85,900	51,555
Southglenn*	Arapahoe	$105,700	43,087
Littleton	Arapahoe	$97,700	33,685

*Census Designated Place. All others are incorporated communities.

Annual Unemployment Rates

Year	Metro Area	National
1985	5.0%	7.2%
1986	6.6%	7.0%
1987	7.0%	6.2%
1988	5.8%	5.5%
1989	5.3%	5.3%
1990	4.5%	5.5%

Major Employment Sectors

Sector	Jobs	Market Share	Average Pay	5-Year Trend
Services	259,000	27%	$21,500	Warm
Wholesale and retail trade	229,800	24%	$12,711	Cold
Government	152,200	16%	$25,213	Cool
Manufacturing	125,100	13%	$31,098	Cold
Transportation and utilities	72,100	8%	n.a.	Warm
Finance, insurance, and real estate	68,900	7%	$26,701	Cold
Construction	36,500	4%	$25,045	Cold

DETROIT

Total Points: 360
Overall Grade: F
National Rank: 70 of 73
Regional Rank: 13 of 14 (Midwest)

Metro Area Report Card

Category	Points	Grade
Economic Momentum	42	C
Future Growth	32	D
Job Opportunities	36	D
Business Opportunities	31	D
Real Estate Opportunities	60	C
Equality of Opportunities	14	D
Overall	360	F

Growth Potential of Metro Area Counties

Rank	County	Population	Per Capita Income	Growth Potential Points	Grade
1.	Livingston	115,645	$19,555	47	B
2.	Washtenaw	282,937	$22,512	44	C+
3.	Oakland	1,083,592	$26,052	35	C
4.	Saint Clair	145,607	$16,087	34	C
5.	Lapeer*	74,768	$15,687	33	C
	Monroe*	133,600	$16,076	33	C
7.	Macomb	717,400	$19,984	27	D
8.	Wayne	2,111,687	$16,955	15	F

*Tied in rank.
Entire metro area is in Michigan.

Biggest Cities

City	County	Median House Price	Population
Detroit	Wayne	$25,600	1,027,974
Warren	Macomb	$69,500	144,864
Sterling Heights	Macomb	$97,000	117,810
Ann Arbor	Washtenaw	$116,400	109,592
Livonia	Wayne	$94,800	100,850
Dearborn	Wayne	$69,600	89,286
Clinton*	Macomb	$87,500	85,866
Westland	Wayne	$63,400	84,724
Southfield	Oakland	$85,100	75,728
Farmington Hills	Oakland	$145,900	74,652

*Census Designated Place. All others are incorporated communities.

Annual Unemployment Rates

Year	Metro Area	National
1985	8.9%	7.2%
1986	8.0%	7.0%
1987	7.9%	6.2%
1988	7.4%	5.5%
1989	6.9%	5.3%
1990	7.3%	5.5%

192 Major Employment Sectors

Sector	Jobs	Market Share	Average Pay	5-Year Trend
Services	560,400	26%	$22,849	Hot
Wholesale and retail trade	505,800	24%	$12,693	Hot
Manufacturing	481,500	23%	$40,049	Cold
Government	289,200	14%	$25,980	Cold
Finance, insurance, and real estate	117,500	6%	$26,305	Warm
Transportation and utilities	94,500	4%	n.a.	Hot
Construction	68,300	3%	$31,535	Hot

EL PASO

Total Points: 346
Overall Grade: F
National Rank: 73 of 73
Regional Rank: 28 of 28 (South)

Metro Area Report Card

Category	Points	Grade
Economic Momentum	31	D
Future Growth	51	C
Job Opportunities	25	F
Business Opportunities	0	F
Real Estate Opportunities	78	B–
Equality of Opportunities	18	C–
Overall	346	F

Growth Potential of Metro Area County

County	Population	Per Capita Income	Growth Potential Points	Grade
El Paso	591,610	$10,735	41	C

Entire metro area is in Texas.

Biggest Cities

City	County	Median House Price	Population
El Paso	El Paso	$58,500	515,342
Socorro	El Paso	$38,800	22,995
Fort Bliss*	El Paso	$46,900	13,915

*Census Designated Place. All others are incorporated communities.

Annual Unemployment Rates

Year	Metro Area	National
1985	10.8%	7.2%
1986	11.5%	7.0%
1987	10.7%	6.2%
1988	10.7%	5.5%
1989	10.2%	5.3%
1990	10.7%	5.5%

Major Employment Sectors

Sector	Jobs	Market Share	Average Pay	5-Year Trend
Wholesale and retail trade	51,900	25%	$11,026	Hot
Government	43,500	21%	$22,208	Hot
Services	43,400	21%	$16,391	Hot
Manufacturing	41,700	20%	$16,364	Hot
Transportation and utilities	10,900	5%	n.a.	Hot
Finance, insurance, and real estate	8,400	4%	$19,209	Cold
Construction	8,000	4%	$15,529	Cold

FRESNO

Total Points: 462
Overall Grade: C
National Rank: 50 of 73
Regional Rank: 13 of 14 (West)

Metro Area Report Card

Category	Points	Grade
Economic Momentum	62	B+
Future Growth	69	B
Job Opportunities	28	F
Business Opportunities	21	F
Real Estate Opportunities	72	C+
Equality of Opportunities	9	F
Overall	462	C

Growth Potential of Metro Area County

County	Population	Per Capita Income	Growth Potential Points	Grade
Fresno	667,490	$15,927	41	C

Entire metro area is in California.

Biggest Cities

City	County	Median House Price	Population
Fresno	Fresno	$80,300	354,202
Clovis	Fresno	$92,300	50,323
Sanger	Fresno	$69,500	16,839

Annual Unemployment Rates

Year	Metro Area	National
1985	12.9%	7.2%
1986	12.3%	7.0%
1987	10.6%	6.2%
1988	10.6%	5.5%
1989	10.0%	5.3%
1990	10.2%	5.5%

Major Employment Sectors

Sector	Jobs	Market Share	Average Pay	5-Year Trend
Wholesale and retail trade	58,900	25%	$13,404	Hot
Services	54,300	23%	$19,062	Hot
Government	51,000	22%	$23,727	Hot
Manufacturing	26,600	11%	$21,742	Hot
Construction	14,500	6%	$23,963	Hot
Finance, insurance, and real estate	13,300	6%	$23,222	Cold
Transportation and utilities	12,900	6%	n.a.	Hot

GRAND RAPIDS

Total Points: 488
Overall Grade: C
National Rank: 44 of 73
Regional Rank: 7 of 14 (Midwest)

Metro Area Report Card

Category	Points	Grade
Economic Momentum	57	B
Future Growth	54	C
Job Opportunities	57	C+
Business Opportunities	37	C–
Real Estate Opportunities	66	C
Equality of Opportunities	17	C–
Overall	488	C

Growth Potential of Metro Area Counties

Rank	County	Population	Per Capita Income	Growth Potential Points	Grade
1.	Ottawa	187,768	$17,196	49	B
2.	Kent	500,631	$17,981	41	C

Entire metro area is in Michigan.

Biggest Cities

City	County	Median House Price	Population
Grand Rapids	Kent	$58,300	189,126
Wyoming	Kent	$57,700	63,891
Kentwood	Kent	$78,100	37,826
Holland	Ottawa	$68,200	30,745

Annual Unemployment Rates

Year	Metro Area	National
1985	8.7%	7.2%
1986	7.4%	7.0%
1987	6.2%	6.2%
1988	5.3%	5.5%
1989	5.2%	5.3%
1990	6.1%	5.5%

Major Employment Sectors

Sector	Jobs	Market Share	Average Pay	5-Year Trend
Manufacturing	102,000	29%	$28,902	Warm
Wholesale and retail trade	96,000	27%	$11,766	Hot
Services	80,700	23%	$18,662	Hot
Government	34,000	10%	$23,578	Warm
Construction	16,800	5%	$26,459	Hot
Finance, insurance, and real estate	16,100	4%	$23,981	Hot
Transportation and utilities	12,300	3%	n.a.	Hot

GREENSBORO

Total Points: 565
Overall Grade: B
National Rank: 21 of 73
Regional Rank: 12 of 28 (South)

Metro Area Report Card

Category	Points	Grade
Economic Momentum	51	C+
Future Growth	59	C+
Job Opportunities	63	B
Business Opportunities	57	B
Real Estate Opportunities	83	B
Equality of Opportunities	27	C
Overall	565	B

Growth Potential of Metro Area Counties

Rank	County	Population	Per Capita Income	Growth Potential Points	Growth Potential Grade
1.	Davidson*	126,677	$14,191	45	B–
	Forsyth*	265,878	$19,655	45	B–
3.	Davie	27,859	$16,770	43	C+
4.	Guilford*	347,420	$19,239	42	C+
	Randolph*	106,546	$14,224	42	C+
	Stokes*	37,223	$13,642	42	C+
7.	Yadkin	30,488	$14,042	38	C

*Tied in rank.
Entire metro area is in North Carolina.

Biggest Cities

City	County	Median House Price	Population
Greensboro	Guilford	$78,500	183,521
Winston-Salem	Forsyth	$69,600	143,485
High Point	Guilford	$65,200	69,496

Annual Unemployment Rates

Year	Metro Area	National
1985	4.5%	7.2%
1986	4.7%	7.0%
1987	3.7%	6.2%
1988	3.0%	5.5%
1989	3.3%	5.3%
1990	3.7%	5.5%

Major Employment Sectors

Sector	Jobs	Market Share	Average Pay	5-Year Trend
Manufacturing	149,500	30%	$24,642	Cool
Wholesale and retail trade	114,400	23%	$12,114	Hot
Services	103,500	21%	$18,282	Hot
Government	55,500	11%	$20,734	Warm
Transportation and utilities	26,300	5%	n.a.	Warm
Construction	24,900	5%	$21,222	Warm
Finance, insurance, and real estate	24,200	5%	$24,463	Warm

GREENVILLE

Total Points: 514
Overall Grade: C
National Rank: 34 of 73
Regional Rank: 18 of 28 (South)

Metro Area Report Card

Category	Points	Grade
Economic Momentum	50	C
Future Growth	53	C
Job Opportunities	65	B
Business Opportunities	49	C
Real Estate Opportunities	84	B+
Equality of Opportunities	7	F
Overall	514	C

Growth Potential of Metro Area Counties

Rank	County	Population	Per Capita Income	Growth Potential Points	Growth Potential Grade
1.	Greenville	320,167	$16,523	47	B
2.	Spartanburg	226,800	$15,304	46	B–
3.	Pickens	93,894	$13,833	45	B–

Entire metro area is in South Carolina.

Biggest Cities

City	County	Median House Price	Population
Greenville	Greenville	$68,700	58,282
Spartanburg	Spartanburg	$58,300	43,467
Wade Hampton*	Greenville	$90,200	20,014

*Census Designated Place. All others are incorporated communities.

Annual Unemployment Rates

Year	Metro Area	National
1985	6.0%	7.2%
1986	5.3%	7.0%
1987	4.4%	6.2%
1988	3.4%	5.5%
1989	3.6%	5.3%
1990	3.9%	5.5%

Major Employment Sectors

Sector	Jobs	Market Share	Average Pay	5-Year Trend
Manufacturing	99,700	30%	$22,991	Warm
Wholesale and retail trade	78,800	23%	$11,522	Hot
Services	64,600	19%	$17,627	Hot
Government	41,700	12%	$21,761	Warm
Construction	25,700	8%	$21,691	Hot
Transportation and utilities	14,600	4%	n.a.	Hot
Finance, insurance, and real estate	12,000	4%	$23,832	Cold

HARRISBURG

Total Points: 514
Overall Grade: C
National Rank: 34 of 73
Regional Rank: 3 of 17 (East)

Metro Area Report Card

Category	Points	Grade
Economic Momentum	32	D+
Future Growth	59	C+
Job Opportunities	60	B–
Business Opportunities	53	C+
Real Estate Opportunities	81	B
Equality of Opportunities	27	C
Overall	514	C

Growth Potential of Metro Area Counties

Rank	County	Population	Per Capita Income	Growth Potential Points	Grade
1.	Cumberland	195,257	$17,873	44	C+
2.	Lebanon	113,744	$15,405	39	C
3.	Dauphin*	237,813	$17,158	36	C
	Perry*	41,172	$13,931	36	C

*Tied in rank.
Entire metro area is in Pennsylvania.

Biggest Cities

City	County	Median House Price	Population
Harrisburg	Dauphin	$38,400	52,376
Lebanon	Lebanon	$45,000	24,800
Carlisle	Cumberland	$77,900	18,419

Annual Unemployment Rates

Year	Metro Area	National
1985	5.6%	7.2%
1986	4.7%	7.0%
1987	4.1%	6.2%
1988	4.0%	5.5%
1989	3.8%	5.3%
1990	4.4%	5.5%

Major Employment Sectors

Sector	Jobs	Market Share	Average Pay	5-Year Trend
Services	71,500	23%	$18,674	Hot
Wholesale and retail trade	70,000	22%	$11,119	Hot
Government	68,400	22%	$24,582	Cold
Manufacturing	49,700	16%	$25,929	Cold
Finance, insurance, and real estate	21,100	7%	$22,332	Hot
Transportation and utilities	20,300	6%	n.a.	Hot
Construction	14,100	4%	$24,658	Hot

HARTFORD

Total Points: 471
Overall Grade: C
National Rank: 46 of 73
Regional Rank: 6 of 17 (East)

Metro Area Report Card

Category	Points	Grade
Economic Momentum	60	B
Future Growth	45	C–
Job Opportunities	56	C+
Business Opportunities	64	B+
Real Estate Opportunities	29	F
Equality of Opportunities	25	C
Overall	471	C

Growth Potential of Metro Area Counties

Rank	County	Population	Per Capita Income	Growth Potential Points	Grade
1.	Middlesex	143,196	$23,542	54	B
2.	Tolland	128,699	$21,563	53	B
3.	Hartford	851,783	$24,040	41	C

Entire metro area is in Connecticut.

Biggest Cities

City	County	Median House Price	Population
Hartford	Hartford	$133,800	139,739
New Britain	Hartford	$139,200	75,491
Bristol	Hartford	$153,500	60,640
West Hartford*	Hartford	$203,300	60,110
East Hartford*	Hartford	$146,200	50,452
Middletown	Middlesex	$157,000	42,762
Central Manchester*	Hartford	$142,400	30,934
Newington*	Hartford	$165,800	29,208
Wethersfield*	Hartford	$185,400	25,651

*Census Designated Places. All others are incorporated communities.

Annual Unemployment Rates

Year	Metro Area	National
1985	4.5%	7.2%
1986	3.3%	7.0%
1987	3.0%	6.2%
1988	2.8%	5.5%
1989	3.3%	5.3%
1990	4.5%	5.5%

The U.S. Bureau of Labor Statistics calculates the unemployment rate for a geographic area that is slightly different from the Hartford metro area defined by this book. Selected towns in the outer portion of the metro area are not included in the above statistics.

ill

Major Employment Sectors

Sector	Jobs	Market Share	Average Pay	5-Year Trend
Services	116,700	24%	$22,899	Warm
Wholesale and retail trade	103,100	22%	$14,773	Cool
Manufacturing	83,400	17%	$33,116	Cold
Finance, insurance, and real estate	75,000	16%	$33,196	Cool
Government	63,600	13%	$29,487	Warm
Transportation and utilities	19,300	4%	n.a.	Hot
Construction	17,000	4%	$33,370	Cool

All figures are for the modified metro area used by the U.S. Bureau of Labor Statistics in its calculations.

HONOLULU

Total Points: 558
Overall Grade: B–
National Rank: 24 of 73
Regional Rank: 9 of 14 (West)

Metro Area Report Card

Category	Points	Grade
Economic Momentum	48	C
Future Growth	40	D
Job Opportunities	73	A–
Business Opportunities	46	C
Real Estate Opportunities	40	D
Equality of Opportunities	79	A
Overall	558	B–

Growth Potential of Metro Area County

County	Population	Per Capita Income	Growth Potential Points	Grade
Honolulu	836,231	$19,171	31	C–

Entire metro area is in Hawaii.

Biggest Cities

City	County	Median House Price	Population
Honolulu*	Honolulu	$353,900	365,272
Kailua*	Honolulu	$318,900	36,818
Kaneohe*	Honolulu	$242,700	35,448
Waipahu*	Honolulu	$234,800	31,435
Pearl City*	Honolulu	$252,300	30,993
Waimalu*	Honolulu	$325,500	29,967
Mililani Town*	Honolulu	$285,300	29,359

*Census Designated Places.

Annual Unemployment Rates

Year	Metro Area	National
1985	5.1%	7.2%
1986	4.4%	7.0%
1987	3.6%	6.2%
1988	2.8%	5.5%
1989	2.2%	5.3%
1990	2.6%	5.5%

Major Employment Sectors

Sector	Jobs	Market Share	Average Pay	5-Year Trend
Services	115,500	28%	$20,785	Hot
Wholesale and retail trade	102,500	25%	$13,654	Warm
Government	87,600	21%	$25,920	Cool
Transportation and utilities	34,200	8%	n.a.	Hot
Finance, insurance, and real estate	29,600	7%	$25,873	Cold
Construction	24,000	6%	$34,896	Hot
Manufacturing	15,800	4%	$23,620	Cool

HOUSTON

Total Points: 408
Overall Grade: D
National Rank: 64 of 73
Regional Rank: 25 of 28 (South)

Metro Area Report Card

Category	Points	Grade
Economic Momentum	27	D
Future Growth	50	C
Job Opportunities	31	D–
Business Opportunities	27	D–
Real Estate Opportunities	54	C–
Equality of Opportunities	54	B
Overall	408	D

Growth Potential of Metro Area Counties

Rank	County	Population	Per Capita Income	Growth Potential Points	Grade
1.	Fort Bend	225,421	$17,164	60	A–
2.	Montgomery	182,201	$14,705	50	B
3.	Galveston	217,399	$16,995	34	C
4.	Brazoria	191,707	$17,099	29	D+
5.	Waller	23,390	$13,051	26	D
6.	Harris	2,818,199	$17,948	23	D
7.	Liberty	52,726	$13,124	21	D–

Entire metro area is in Texas.

Biggest Cities

City	County	Median House Price	Population
Houston	Harris	$58,000	1,630,553
Pasadena	Harris	$49,000	119,363
Baytown	Harris	$50,400	63,850
Galveston	Galveston	$57,200	59,070
Texas City	Galveston	$50,300	40,822
Kingwood*	Harris	$116,700	37,397
Missouri City	Fort Bend	$79,000	36,176
Spring*	Harris	$54,600	33,111
League City	Galveston	$69,100	30,159
The Woodlands*	Montgomery	$101,800	29,205

*Census Designated Places. All others are incorporated communities.

Annual Unemployment Rates

Year	Metro Area	National
1985	8.0%	7.2%
1986	10.4%	7.0%
1987	9.1%	6.2%
1988	7.0%	5.5%
1989	6.0%	5.3%
1990	5.3%	5.5%

212   Major Employment Sectors

Sector	Jobs	Market Share	Average Pay	5-Year Trend
Services	477,100	27%	$22,880	Hot
Wholesale and retail trade	400,800	23%	$12,607	Cold
Government	241,100	14%	$22,617	Warm
Manufacturing	199,200	11%	$33,050	Cool
Construction	122,900	7%	$26,711	Cool
Transportation and utilities	117,600	7%	n.a.	Warm
Finance, insurance, and real estate	109,100	6%	$27,635	Cold

INDIANAPOLIS

Total Points: 560
Overall Grade: B–
National Rank: 22 of 73
Regional Rank: 1 of 14 (Midwest)

Metro Area Report Card

Category	Points	Grade
Economic Momentum	45	C
Future Growth	60	C+
Job Opportunities	66	B
Business Opportunities	51	C+
Real Estate Opportunities	77	B–
Equality of Opportunities	39	B–
Overall	560	B–

Growth Potential of Metro Area Counties

Rank	County	Population	Per Capita Income	Growth Potential Points	Grade
1.	Hamilton	108,936	$23,928	59	B+
2.	Johnson	88,109	$17,562	42	C+
3.	Hendricks	75,717	$17,361	35	C
4.	Morgan	55,920	$14,822	33	C
5.	Boone*	38,147	$20,025	31	C–
	Hancock*	45,527	$17,328	31	C–
7.	Shelby	40,307	$15,509	27	D
8.	Marion	797,159	$17,730	21	D–

*Tied in rank.
Entire metro area is in Indiana.

Biggest Cities

City	County	Median House Price	Population
Indianapolis	Marion	$60,800	731,327
Lawrence	Marion	$64,400	26,763
Greenwood	Johnson	$74,400	26,265
Carmel	Hamilton	$142,500	25,380

Annual Unemployment Rates

Year	Metro Area	National
1985	6.1%	7.2%
1986	5.1%	7.0%
1987	5.2%	6.2%
1988	4.6%	5.5%
1989	4.0%	5.3%
1990	4.2%	5.5%

Major Employment Sectors

Sector	Jobs	Market Share	Average Pay	5-Year Trend
Wholesale and retail trade	171,800	26%	$11,809	Hot
Services	158,400	24%	$19,505	Hot
Manufacturing	110,300	16%	$31,174	Warm
Government	99,000	15%	$23,653	Warm
Finance, insurance, and real estate	49,700	7%	$24,187	Hot
Transportation and utilities	43,500	6%	n.a.	Hot
Construction	37,800	6%	$24,568	Hot

JACKSONVILLE

Total Points: 595
Overall Grade: B
National Rank: 16 of 73
Regional Rank: 9 of 28 (South)

Metro Area Report Card

Category	Points	Grade
Economic Momentum	49	C
Future Growth	78	A–
Job Opportunities	59	B–
Business Opportunities	59	B
Real Estate Opportunities	82	B
Equality of Opportunities	17	C–
Overall	595	B

Growth Potential of Metro Area Counties

Rank	County	Population	Per Capita Income	Growth Potential Points	Growth Potential Grade
1.	Saint Johns	83,829	$18,436	68	A
2.	Clay	105,986	$15,785	67	A
3.	Nassau	43,941	$15,316	47	B
4.	Duval	672,971	$16,074	44	C+

Entire metro area is in Florida.

Biggest Cities

City	County	Median House Price	Population
Jacksonville	Duval	$62,900	635,230
Lakeside*	Clay	$88,100	29,137
Jacksonville Beach	Duval	$73,500	17,839

*Census Designated Place. All others are incorporated communities.

Annual Unemployment Rates

Year	Metro Area	National
1985	5.2%	7.2%
1986	5.4%	7.0%
1987	5.3%	6.2%
1988	5.3%	5.5%
1989	5.7%	5.3%
1990	5.5%	5.5%

Major Employment Sectors

Sector	Jobs	Market Share	Average Pay	5-Year Trend
Services	114,000	27%	$19,231	Hot
Wholesale and retail trade	113,200	27%	$12,275	Hot
Government	63,900	15%	$23,320	Hot
Finance, insurance, and real estate	42,200	10%	$25,250	Hot
Manufacturing	36,400	9%	$24,937	Cool
Transportation and utilities	29,200	7%	n.a.	Cool
Construction	26,100	6%	$20,824	Cold

KANSAS CITY

Total Points: 543
Overall Grade: C+
National Rank: 26 of 73
Regional Rank: 2 of 14 (Midwest)

Metro Area Report Card

Category	Points	Grade
Economic Momentum	31	D
Future Growth	64	B–
Job Opportunities	53	C
Business Opportunities	54	B–
Real Estate Opportunities	82	B
Equality of Opportunities	46	B
Overall	543	C+

Growth Potential of Metro Area Counties

Rank	County	Population	Per Capita Income	Growth Potential Points	Grade
1.	Johnson, Kan.	355,054	$23,346	50	B
2.	Platte	57,867	$18,329	45	B–
3.	Clay	153,411	$17,979	42	C+
4.	Cass	63,808	$15,827	41	C
5.	Leavenworth, Kan.	64,371	$12,674	35	C
6.	Jackson	633,232	$17,328	29	D+
7.	Lafayette*	31,107	$15,385	25	D
	Miami, Kan.*	23,466	$14,064	25	D
9.	Ray*	21,971	$14,540	24	D
	Wyandotte, Kan.*	161,993	$12,752	24	D

*Tied in rank.

Biggest Cities

City	County	Median House Price	Population
Kansas City, Mo.	Jackson	$56,100	435,146
Kansas City, Kan.	Wyandotte	$41,200	149,767
Independence	Jackson	$56,000	112,301
Overland Park, Kan.	Johnson	$95,300	111,790
Olathe, Kan.	Johnson	$83,300	63,352
Lee's Summit	Jackson	$84,700	46,418
Blue Springs	Jackson	$76,700	40,153
Leavenworth, Kan.	Leavenworth	$57,500	38,495
Shawnee, Kan.	Johnson	$84,800	37,993
Lenexa, Kan.	Johnson	$104,000	34,034

Cities are in Missouri unless otherwise indicated. State names are listed with each Kansas City to prevent confusion.

Annual Unemployment Rates

Year	Metro Area	National
1985	4.7%	7.2%
1986	4.6%	7.0%
1987	5.6%	6.2%
1988	5.3%	5.5%
1989	4.9%	5.3%
1990	5.0%	5.5%

Major Employment Sectors

Sector	Jobs	Market Share	Average Pay	5-Year Trend
Wholesale and retail trade	200,100	26%	$11,940	Cool
Services	197,100	25%	$19,561	Hot
Government	121,400	15%	$23,282	Warm
Manufacturing	109,800	14%	$29,295	Cold
Transportation and utilities	63,100	8%	n.a.	Hot
Finance, insurance, and real estate	59,500	8%	$24,853	Warm
Construction	32,600	4%	$25,978	Cool

KNOXVILLE

Total Points: 635
Overall Grade: B+
National Rank: 8 of 73
Regional Rank: 4 of 28 (South)

Metro Area Report Card

Category	Points	Grade
Economic Momentum	49	C
Future Growth	68	B
Job Opportunities	50	C
Business Opportunities	79	A
Real Estate Opportunities	89	A
Equality of Opportunities	29	C
Overall	635	B+

Growth Potential of Metro Area Counties

Rank	County	Population	Per Capita Income	Growth Potential Points	Grade
1.	Sevier	51,043	$12,663	42	C+
2.	Knox	335,749	$16,538	40	C
3.	Union	13,694	$9,675	38	C
4.	Blount	85,969	$14,192	36	C
5.	Jefferson	33,016	$12,006	35	C
6.	Anderson*	68,250	$15,126	32	C–
	Grainger*	17,095	$9,534	32	C–

*Tied in rank.
Entire metro area is in Tennessee.

Biggest Cities

City	County	Median House Price	Population
Knoxville	Knox	$49,800	165,121
Oak Ridge	Anderson	$64,100	27,310
Maryville	Blount	$64,900	19,208

Annual Unemployment Rates

Year	Metro Area	National
1985	7.4%	7.2%
1986	7.8%	7.0%
1987	6.4%	6.2%
1988	5.5%	5.5%
1989	5.4%	5.3%
1990	5.0%	5.5%

Major Employment Sectors

Sector	Jobs	Market Share	Average Pay	5-Year Trend
Wholesale and retail trade	70,200	26%	$10,805	Hot
Services	58,000	22%	$18,600	Warm
Government	51,900	19%	$22,258	Cool
Manufacturing	50,200	19%	$24,044	Cool
Construction	13,500	5%	$20,483	Hot
Transportation and utilities	11,400	4%	n.a.	Hot
Finance, insurance, and real estate	10,200	4%	$20,819	Warm

LAS VEGAS

Total Points: 730
Overall Grade: A
National Rank: 3 of 73
Regional Rank: 1 of 14 (West)

Metro Area Report Card

Category	Points	Grade
Economic Momentum	94	A+
Future Growth	93	A+
Job Opportunities	80	A
Business Opportunities	22	F
Real Estate Opportunities	76	C+
Equality of Opportunities	16	D+
Overall	730	A

Growth Potential of Metro Area County

County	Population	Per Capita Income	Growth Potential Points	Grade
Clark	741,459	$18,508	60	A–

Entire metro area is in Nevada.

Biggest Cities

City	County	Median House Price	Population
Las Vegas	Clark	$89,200	258,295
Paradise*	Clark	$102,300	124,682
Sunrise Manor*	Clark	$84,900	95,362
Henderson	Clark	$100,700	64,942
Spring Valley*	Clark	$112,900	51,726
North Las Vegas	Clark	$58,100	47,707
Winchester*	Clark	$93,900	23,365

*Census Designated Places. All others are incorporated communities.

Annual Unemployment Rates

Year	Metro Area	National
1985	8.6%	7.2%
1986	6.2%	7.0%
1987	6.5%	6.2%
1988	5.4%	5.5%
1989	5.0%	5.3%
1990	4.9%	5.5%

Major Employment Sectors

Sector	Jobs	Market Share	Average Pay	5-Year Trend
Services	177,600	47%	$20,259	Hot
Wholesale and retail trade	76,100	20%	$13,713	Hot
Government	39,100	10%	$26,952	Hot
Construction	35,500	9%	$26,748	Hot
Transportation and utilities	19,300	5%	n.a.	Hot
Finance, insurance, and real estate	18,400	5%	$23,220	Hot
Manufacturing	10,700	3%	$24,624	Hot

LITTLE ROCK

Total Points: 560
Overall Grade: B–
National Rank: 22 of 73
Regional Rank: 13 of 28 (South)

Metro Area Report Card

Category	Points	Grade
Economic Momentum	35	C–
Future Growth	62	B–
Job Opportunities	47	C
Business Opportunities	65	B+
Real Estate Opportunities	92	A
Equality of Opportunities	30	C
Overall	560	B–

Growth Potential of Metro Area Counties

Rank	County	Population	Per Capita Income	Growth Potential Points	Grade
1.	Faulkner	60,006	$13,699	46	B–
2.	Pulaski	349,660	$16,685	39	C
3.	Saline	64,183	$13,445	36	C
4.	Lonoke	39,268	$12,725	34	C

Entire metro area is in Arkansas.

Biggest Cities

City	County	Median House Price	Population
Little Rock	Pulaski	$64,200	175,795
North Little Rock	Pulaski	$56,100	61,741
Jacksonville	Pulaski	$55,100	29,101
Conway	Faulkner	$63,100	26,481

Annual Unemployment Rates

Year	Metro Area	National
1985	6.3%	7.2%
1986	6.9%	7.0%
1987	7.2%	6.2%
1988	6.4%	5.5%
1989	6.3%	5.3%
1990	5.9%	5.5%

Major Employment Sectors

Sector	Jobs	Market Share	Average Pay	5-Year Trend
Services	66,600	26%	$18,203	Hot
Wholesale and retail trade	61,100	24%	$11,699	Hot
Government	49,000	19%	$21,551	Cool
Manufacturing	33,300	13%	$21,740	Cool
Transportation and utilities	16,500	7%	n.a.	Warm
Finance, insurance, and real estate	15,600	6%	$25,479	Cold
Construction	11,000	4%	$19,348	Cold

LOS ANGELES

Total Points: 522
Overall Grade: C+
National Rank: 31 of 73
Regional Rank: 11 of 14 (West)

Metro Area Report Card

Category	Points	Grade
Economic Momentum	56	B–
Future Growth	68	B
Job Opportunities	58	C+
Business Opportunities	30	D
Real Estate Opportunities	35	D–
Equality of Opportunities	56	B
Overall	522	C+

Growth Potential of Metro Area Counties

Rank	County	Population	Per Capita Income	Growth Potential Points	Grade
1.	Riverside	1,170,413	$17,028	65	A
2.	San Bernardino	1,418,380	$15,635	55	B
3.	Ventura	669,016	$20,156	54	B
4.	Orange	2,410,556	$24,288	35	C
5.	Los Angeles	8,863,164	$19,906	28	D

Entire metro area is in California.

Biggest Cities

City	County	Median House Price	Population
Los Angeles	Los Angeles	$244,500	3,485,398
Long Beach	Los Angeles	$222,900	429,433
Santa Ana	Orange	$185,400	293,742
Anaheim	Orange	$218,700	266,406
Riverside	Riverside	$134,800	226,505
Huntington Beach	Orange	$287,100	181,519
Glendale	Los Angeles	$343,600	180,038
San Bernardino	San Bernardino	$96,200	164,164
Garden Grove	Orange	$199,700	143,050
Oxnard	Ventura	$204,600	142,216

Annual Unemployment Rates

Year	Metro Area	National
1985	6.6%	7.2%
1986	6.1%	7.0%
1987	5.3%	6.2%
1988	4.7%	5.5%
1989	4.5%	5.3%
1990	5.4%	5.5%

Major Employment Sectors

Sector	Jobs	Market Share	Average Pay	5-Year Trend
Services	1,808,200	28%	$25,098	Hot
Wholesale and retail trade	1,517,700	23%	$14,897	Hot
Manufacturing	1,234,400	19%	$29,022	Cool
Government	857,700	13%	$28,441	Warm
Finance, insurance, and real estate	440,100	7%	$32,456	Hot
Construction	314,800	5%	$27,861	Hot
Transportation and utilities	307,100	5%	n.a.	Hot

LOUISVILLE

Total Points: 520
Overall Grade: C
National Rank: 33 of 73
Regional Rank: 17 of 28 (South)

Metro Area Report Card

Category	Points	Grade
Economic Momentum	34	C–
Future Growth	52	C
Job Opportunities	50	C
Business Opportunities	46	C
Real Estate Opportunities	93	A
Equality of Opportunities	33	C
Overall	520	C

Growth Potential of Metro Area Counties

Rank	County	Population	Per Capita Income	Growth Potential Points	Grade
1.	Oldham	33,263	$15,060	46	B–
2.	Floyd, Ind.	64,404	$15,732	39	C
3.	Bullitt	47,567	$12,513	38	C
4.	Clark, Ind.*	87,777	$14,529	31	C–
	Shelby*	24,824	$15,059	31	C–
6.	Harrison, Ind.	29,890	$13,365	30	C–
7.	Jefferson	664,937	$17,783	21	D–

*Tied in rank.
Counties are in Kentucky unless otherwise indicated.

Biggest Cities

City	County	Median House Price	Population
Louisville	Jefferson	$44,300	269,063
New Albany, Ind.	Floyd	$48,100	36,322
Pleasure Ridge Park*	Jefferson	$49,100	25,131
Jeffersontown	Jefferson	$73,400	23,221
Valley Station*	Jefferson	$47,800	22,840
Jeffersonville, Ind.	Clark	$45,700	21,841
Newburg*	Jefferson	$40,500	21,647

*Census Designated Places. All others are incorporated communities.
Cities are in Kentucky unless otherwise indicated.

Annual Unemployment Rates

Year	Metro Area	National
1985	8.0%	7.2%
1986	7.0%	7.0%
1987	6.9%	6.2%
1988	6.3%	5.5%
1989	5.6%	5.3%
1990	5.1%	5.5%

230   Major Employment Sectors

Sector	Jobs	Market Share	Average Pay	5-Year Trend
Services	124,800	26%	$17,104	Hot
Wholesale and retail trade	119,500	25%	$10,923	Hot
Manufacturing	89,000	19%	$28,757	Warm
Government	63,700	13%	$22,904	Cool
Transportation and utilities	31,000	6%	n.a.	Hot
Finance, insurance, and real estate	27,800	6%	$25,052	Cold
Construction	23,500	5%	$21,180	Hot

MEMPHIS

Total Points: 498
Overall Grade: C
National Rank: 41 of 73
Regional Rank: 21 of 28 (South)

Metro Area Report Card

Category	Points	Grade
Economic Momentum	50	C
Future Growth	64	B–
Job Opportunities	54	C
Business Opportunities	34	C–
Real Estate Opportunities	85	B+
Equality of Opportunities	7	F
Overall	498	C

Growth Potential of Metro Area Counties

Rank	County	Population	Per Capita Income	Growth Potential Points	Grade
1.	DeSoto, Miss.	67,910	$13,633	45	B–
2.	Shelby	826,330	$17,301	36	C
3.	Tipton	37,568	$11,919	35	C
4.	Crittenden, Ark.	49,939	$10,940	24	D

Counties are in Tennessee unless otherwise indicated.

Biggest Cities

City	County	Median House Price	Population
Memphis	Shelby	$55,700	610,337
Germantown	Shelby	$145,100	32,893
West Memphis, Ark.	Crittenden	$50,900	28,259
Bartlett	Shelby	$91,200	26,989

Cities are in Tennessee unless otherwise indicated.

Annual Unemployment Rates

Year	Metro Area	National
1985	6.6%	7.2%
1986	6.8%	7.0%
1987	5.7%	6.2%
1988	5.1%	5.5%
1989	4.7%	5.3%
1990	4.6%	5.5%

Major Employment Sectors

Sector	Jobs	Market Share	Average Pay	5-Year Trend
Wholesale and retail trade	125,600	26%	$11,705	Warm
Services	120,200	25%	$18,649	Hot
Government	75,700	16%	$21,946	Cool
Manufacturing	62,300	13%	$25,872	Hot
Transportation and utilities	47,300	10%	n.a.	Hot
Finance, insurance, and real estate	25,100	5%	$25,979	Cold
Construction	20,200	4%	$22,091	Cool

MIAMI

Total Points: 632
Overall Grade: B+
National Rank: 10 of 73
Regional Rank: 6 of 28 (South)

Metro Area Report Card

Category	Points	Grade
Economic Momentum	50	C
Future Growth	38	D
Job Opportunities	53	C
Business Opportunities	89	A
Real Estate Opportunities	64	C
Equality of Opportunities	78	A
Overall	632	B+

Growth Potential of Metro Area Counties

Rank	County	Population	Per Capita Income	Growth Potential Points	Grade
1.	Broward	1,255,488	$21,898	50	B
2.	Dade	1,937,094	$17,963	42	C+

Entire metro area is in Florida.

Biggest Cities

City	County	Median House Price	Population
Miami	Dade	$79,200	358,548
Hialeah	Dade	$80,100	188,004
Fort Lauderdale	Broward	$99,200	149,377
Hollywood	Broward	$82,100	121,697
Miami Beach	Dade	$191,300	92,639
Kendall*	Dade	$143,700	87,271
Coral Springs	Broward	$160,200	79,443
Pompano Beach	Broward	$99,300	72,411
Plantation	Broward	$130,100	66,692
Pembroke Pines	Broward	$93,800	65,452

*Census Designated Place. All others are incorporated communities.

Annual Unemployment Rates

Year	Metro Area	National
1985	6.5%	7.2%
1986	5.8%	7.0%
1987	5.2%	6.2%
1988	4.9%	5.5%
1989	5.9%	5.3%
1990	6.2%	5.5%

Major Employment Sectors

Sector	Jobs	Market Share	Average Pay	5-Year Trend
Services	408,400	29%	$21,986	Hot
Wholesale and retail trade	391,800	28%	$13,676	Hot
Government	190,400	14%	$26,034	Hot
Manufacturing	132,300	9%	$21,941	Cold
Finance, insurance, and real estate	111,200	8%	$26,698	Cool
Transportation and utilities	95,800	7%	n.a.	Warm
Construction	72,500	5%	$22,947	Cold

MILWAUKEE

Total Points: 380
Overall Grade: D–
National Rank: 68 of 73
Regional Rank: 12 of 14 (Midwest)

Metro Area Report Card

Category	Points	Grade
Economic Momentum	31	D
Future Growth	33	D
Job Opportunities	56	C+
Business Opportunities	46	C
Real Estate Opportunities	59	C
Equality of Opportunities	7	F
Overall	380	D–

Growth Potential of Metro Area Counties

Rank	County	Population	Per Capita Income	Growth Potential Points	Growth Potential Grade
1.	Ozaukee	72,831	$22,373	43	C+
2.	Washington*	95,328	$17,734	41	C
	Waukesha*	304,715	$20,691	41	C
4.	Racine	175,034	$17,426	32	C–
5.	Milwaukee	959,275	$18,062	16	F

*Tied in rank.
Entire metro area is in Wisconsin.

Biggest Cities

City	County	Median House Price	Population
Milwaukee	Milwaukee	$53,500	628,088
Racine	Racine	$52,300	84,298
West Allis	Milwaukee	$63,100	63,221
Waukesha	Waukesha	$81,600	56,958
Wauwatosa	Milwaukee	$89,300	49,366
Brookfield	Waukesha	$121,900	35,184
New Berlin	Waukesha	$96,700	33,592
Greenfield	Milwaukee	$80,300	33,403
Menomonee Falls	Waukesha	$87,600	26,840
West Bend	Washington	$73,100	23,916

Annual Unemployment Rates

Year	Metro Area	National
1985	6.7%	7.2%
1986	6.4%	7.0%
1987	5.5%	6.2%
1988	3.8%	5.5%
1989	3.9%	5.3%
1990	3.9%	5.5%

Major Employment Sectors

Sector	Jobs	Market Share	Average Pay	5-Year Trend
Services	226,100	27%	$18,570	Hot
Manufacturing	200,700	24%	$28,973	Warm
Wholesale and retail trade	189,800	23%	$10,809	Hot
Government	94,100	11%	$25,675	Cool
Finance, insurance, and real estate	52,700	6%	$25,353	Cool
Transportation and utilities	39,500	5%	n.a.	Cool
Construction	28,400	3%	$28,395	Hot

MINNEAPOLIS

Total Points: 527
Overall Grade: C+
National Rank: 29 of 73
Regional Rank: 3 of 14 (Midwest)

Metro Area Report Card

Category	Points	Grade
Economic Momentum	42	C
Future Growth	59	C+
Job Opportunities	59	B–
Business Opportunities	45	C
Real Estate Opportunities	57	C
Equality of Opportunities	52	B
Overall	527	C+

Growth Potential of Metro Area Counties

Rank	County	Population	Per Capita Income	Growth Potential Points	Growth Potential Grade
1.	Dakota	275,227	$20,082	63	A
2.	Washington	145,896	$19,886	58	B+
3.	Scott	57,846	$18,180	52	B
4.	Anoka*	243,641	$16,578	50	B
	Carver*	47,915	$18,902	50	B
6.	Saint Croix, Wis.	50,251	$18,055	43	C+
7.	Chisago*	30,521	$14,994	40	C
	Wright*	68,710	$14,788	40	C
9.	Isanti	25,921	$13,812	33	C
10.	Hennepin	1,032,431	$22,584	28	D
11.	Ramsey	485,765	$19,337	21	D–

*Tied in rank.
Counties are in Minnesota unless otherwise indicated.

Biggest Cities

City	County	Median House Price	Population
Minneapolis	Hennepin	$71,700	368,383
Saint Paul	Ramsey	$70,900	272,235
Bloomington	Hennepin	$97,500	86,335
Brooklyn Park	Hennepin	$88,400	56,381
Coon Rapids	Anoka	$82,500	52,978
Burnsville	Dakota	$108,100	51,288
Plymouth	Hennepin	$127,400	50,889
Minnetonka	Hennepin	$121,000	48,370
Eagan	Dakota	$104,300	47,409
Edina	Hennepin	$156,700	46,070

Annual Unemployment Rates

Year	Metro Area	National
1985	4.6%	7.2%
1986	4.2%	7.0%
1987	4.4%	6.2%
1988	3.4%	5.5%
1989	3.8%	5.3%
1990	4.3%	5.5%

Major Employment Sectors

Sector	Jobs	Market Share	Average Pay	5-Year Trend
Services	369,800	27%	$19,964	Hot
Wholesale and retail trade	329,200	24%	$12,344	Warm
Manufacturing	260,500	19%	$32,433	Cool
Government	186,300	14%	$27,024	Warm
Finance, insurance, and real estate	96,900	7%	$28,909	Cool
Transportation and utilities	76,700	6%	n.a.	Hot
Construction	49,800	4%	$30,702	Cool

NASHVILLE

Total Points: 624
Overall Grade: B+
National Rank: 11 of 73
Regional Rank: 7 of 28 (South)

Metro Area Report Card

Category	Points	Grade
Economic Momentum	54	B–
Future Growth	69	B
Job Opportunities	64	B
Business Opportunities	64	B+
Real Estate Opportunities	82	B
Equality of Opportunities	42	B
Overall	624	B+

Growth Potential of Metro Area Counties

Rank	County	Population	Per Capita Income	Growth Potential Points	Growth Potential Grade
1.	Rutherford*	118,570	$14,859	59	B+
	Williamson*	81,021	$22,097	59	B+
3.	Sumner	103,281	$15,291	47	B
4.	Cheatham	27,140	$13,129	45	B–
5.	Wilson	67,675	$15,413	44	C+
6.	Dickson	35,061	$13,817	40	C
7.	Davidson	510,784	$18,359	38	C
8.	Robertson	41,494	$12,142	36	C

*Tied in rank.
Entire metro area is in Tennessee.

Biggest Cities

City	County	Median House Price	Population
Nashville	Davidson	$74,400	488,374
Murfreesboro	Rutherford	$78,200	44,922
Hendersonville	Sumner	$86,300	32,188
Franklin	Williamson	$95,900	20,098

Annual Unemployment Rates

Year	Metro Area	National
1985	4.7%	7.2%
1986	4.9%	7.0%
1987	4.4%	6.2%
1988	4.4%	5.5%
1989	3.8%	5.3%
1990	4.0%	5.5%

Major Employment Sectors

Sector	Jobs	Market Share	Average Pay	5-Year Trend
Services	138,200	28%	$20,080	Hot
Wholesale and retail trade	123,600	25%	$12,799	Hot
Manufacturing	89,400	18%	$25,328	Cool
Government	69,000	14%	$22,580	Cool
Finance, insurance, and real estate	30,900	6%	$24,800	Cold
Transportation and utilities	26,900	5%	n.a.	Hot
Construction	24,600	5%	$22,027	Cold

NEW HAVEN

Total Points: 429
Overall Grade: C–
National Rank: 57 of 73
Regional Rank: 12 of 17 (East)

Metro Area Report Card

Category	Points	Grade
Economic Momentum	58	B
Future Growth	26	F
Job Opportunities	56	C+
Business Opportunities	64	B+
Real Estate Opportunities	31	F
Equality of Opportunities	23	C
Overall	429	C–

Growth Potential of Metro Area County

County	Population	Per Capita Income	Growth Potential Points	Growth Potential Grade
New Haven	804,219	$21,736	40	C

Entire metro area is in Connecticut.

Biggest Cities

City	County	Median House Price	Population
New Haven	New Haven	$145,000	130,474
Waterbury	New Haven	$131,800	108,961
Meriden	New Haven	$146,300	59,479
West Haven	New Haven	$147,000	54,021
Milford	New Haven	$172,400	49,938
Naugatuck	New Haven	$143,100	30,625
East Haven*	New Haven	$144,600	26,144
North Haven*	New Haven	$189,400	22,249

*Census Designated Places. All others are incorporated communities.

Annual Unemployment Rates

Year	Metro Area	National
1985	4.9%	7.2%
1986	3.7%	7.0%
1987	3.2%	6.2%
1988	2.9%	5.5%
1989	3.5%	5.3%
1990	4.9%	5.5%

The U.S. Bureau of Labor Statistics calculates the unemployment rate for a geographic area that is slightly different from the New Haven metro area defined by this book. Selected towns in the outer portion of the metro area are not included in the above statistics.

Major Employment Sectors

Sector	Jobs	Market Share	Average Pay	5-Year Trend
Services	81,700	32%	$22,500	Hot
Wholesale and retail trade	55,800	22%	$14,799	Cold
Manufacturing	44,400	17%	$29,010	Cold
Government	32,100	12%	$27,391	Cool
Transportation and utilities	17,500	7%	n.a.	Cold
Finance, insurance, and real estate	16,900	7%	$27,226	Hot
Construction	10,400	4%	$32,338	Cold

All figures are for the modified metro area used by the U.S. Bureau of Labor Statistics in its calculations.

NEW ORLEANS

Total Points: 355
Overall Grade: F
National Rank: 71 of 73
Regional Rank: 27 of 28 (South)

Metro Area Report Card

Category	Points	Grade
Economic Momentum	7	F
Future Growth	41	D+
Job Opportunities	13	F
Business Opportunities	41	C
Real Estate Opportunities	87	A–
Equality of Opportunities	25	C
Overall	355	F

Growth Potential of Metro Area Parishes

Rank	Parish	Population	Per Capita Income	Growth Potential Points	Grade
1.	Saint Tammany	144,508	$14,702	42	C+
2.	Saint John the Baptist	39,996	$11,918	34	C
3.	Saint Charles	42,437	$14,484	29	D+
4.	Jefferson	448,306	$15,235	23	D
5.	Saint Bernard	66,631	$12,665	22	D–
6.	Orleans	496,938	$14,838	10	F

Entire metro area is in Louisiana.

Biggest Cities

City	Parish	Median House Price	Population
New Orleans	Orleans	$69,600	496,938
Metairie*	Jefferson	$86,500	149,428
Kenner	Jefferson	$74,200	72,033
Marrero*	Jefferson	$54,600	36,671
Chalmette*	Saint Bernard	$66,600	31,860
Laplace*	Saint John the Baptist	$67,300	24,194
Slidell	Saint Tammany	$67,800	24,124
Terrytown*	Jefferson	$69,100	23,787
Harvey*	Jefferson	$60,000	21,222

*Census Designated Places. All others are incorporated communities.

Annual Unemployment Rates

Year	Metro Area	National
1985	10.9%	7.2%
1986	10.9%	7.0%
1987	10.1%	6.2%
1988	9.5%	5.5%
1989	7.1%	5.3%
1990	5.7%	5.5%

248   Major Employment Sectors

Sector	Jobs	Market Share	Average Pay	5-Year Trend
Services	154,300	29%	$18,933	Cool
Wholesale and retail trade	133,600	25%	$11,148	Cold
Government	90,100	17%	$20,758	Cold
Manufacturing	44,700	8%	$27,609	Cool
Transportation and utilities	43,900	8%	n.a.	Cold
Finance, insurance, and real estate	31,700	6%	$24,025	Cold
Construction	23,000	4%	$22,776	Cold

NEW YORK CITY

Total Points: 381
Overall Grade: D–
National Rank: 67 of 73
Regional Rank: 16 of 17 (East)

Metro Area Report Card

Category	Points	Grade
Economic Momentum	58	B
Future Growth	13	F
Job Opportunities	42	C–
Business Opportunities	63	B
Real Estate Opportunities	14	F
Equality of Opportunities	37	C+
Overall	381	D–

Growth Potential of Metro Area Counties

Rank	County	Population	Per Capita Income	Growth Potential Points	Growth Potential Grade
1.	Hunterdon, N.J.	107,776	$30,301	63	A
2.	Ocean, N.J.	433,203	$20,844	59	B+
3.	Somerset, N.J.	240,279	$32,469	57	B+
4.	Orange	307,647	$19,178	54	B
5.	Sussex, N.J.	130,943	$23,782	53	B
6.	Putnam	83,941	$24,760	51	B
7.	Morris, N.J.	421,353	$29,981	45	B–
8.	Monmouth, N.J.	553,124	$25,393	44	C+
9.	Fairfield, Conn.	827,645	$31,438	39	C
10.	Suffolk	1,321,864	$22,601	38	C
11.	Middlesex, N.J.	671,780	$24,139	35	C
12.	Rockland	265,475	$25,094	34	C
13.	New York (Manhattan)	1,487,536	$35,193	30	C–
14.	Richmond (Staten Island)*	378,977	$21,746	29	D+
	Westchester*	874,866	$31,188	29	D+
16.	Bergen, N.J.	825,380	$30,967	26	D
17.	Passaic, N.J.	453,060	$20,977	25	D
18.	Essex, N.J.*	778,206	$21,873	23	D
	Hudson, N.J.*	553,099	$18,440	23	D
	Nassau*	1,287,348	$28,678	23	D
	Union, N.J.*	493,819	$25,328	23	D
22.	Bronx (Bronx)*	1,203,789	$14,234	21	D–
	Kings (Brooklyn)*	2,300,664	$15,683	21	D–
24.	Queens (Queens)	1,951,598	$19,835	20	F

*Tied in rank.
Counties are in New York unless otherwise indicated.

Biggest Cities

City	County	Median House Price	Population
New York City	†	$189,600	7,322,564
Newark, N.J.	Essex	$110,000	275,221
Jersey City, N.J.	Hudson	$127,700	228,537
Yonkers	Westchester	$228,100	188,082
Bridgeport, Conn.	Fairfield	$145,900	141,686
Paterson, N.J.	Passaic	$138,700	140,891
Elizabeth, N.J.	Union	$145,400	110,002
Stamford, Conn.	Fairfield	$295,700	108,056
Edison, N.J.*	Middlesex	$186,200	88,680
Norwalk, Conn.	Fairfield	$241,300	78,331

*Census Designated Place. All others are incorporated communities.
Cities are in New York unless otherwise indicated.
†New York City consists of the boroughs of the Bronx, Brooklyn (Kings County),
Manhattan (New York County), Queens, and Staten Island (Richmond County).

Annual Unemployment Rates

Year	Metro Area	National
1985	6.2%	7.2%
1986	5.7%	7.0%
1987	4.4%	6.2%
1988	3.9%	5.5%
1989	4.7%	5.3%
1990	5.4%	5.5%

Unemployment statistics for Fairfield County, Conn., were not available from the U.S. Bureau of Labor Statistics. The above figures are for the remainder of the metro area.

Major Employment Sectors

Sector	Jobs	Market Share	Average Pay	5-Year Trend
Services	2,369,100	29%	$26,419	Cool
Wholesale and retail trade	1,703,100	21%	$15,936	Cold
Government	1,291,300	16%	$29,748	Cool
Manufacturing	1,041,500	13%	$32,039	Cold
Finance, insurance, and real estate	830,500	10%	$42,645	Cool
Transportation and utilities	505,000	6%	n.a.	Cold
Construction	306,800	4%	$33,619	Cool

Statistics for Fairfield County, Conn., were not available from the U.S. Bureau of Labor Statistics. The above figures are for the remainder of the metro area.

NORFOLK

Total Points: 447
Overall Grade: C–
National Rank: 52 of 73
Regional Rank: 23 of 28 (South)

Metro Area Report Card

Category	Points	Grade
Economic Momentum	39	C
Future Growth	53	C
Job Opportunities	58	C+
Business Opportunities	31	D
Real Estate Opportunities	71	C
Equality of Opportunities	12	D–
Overall	447	C–

Growth Potential of Metro Area Counties

Rank	County	Population	Per Capita Income	Growth Potential Points	Grade
1.	James City	34,859	$15,429§	77	A
2.	Chesapeake†	151,976	$15,709	60	A–
3.	Gloucester*	30,131	$14,844	55	B
	York*	42,422	$18,357§	55	B
	Virginia Beach†*	393,069	$17,383	55	B
6.	Poquoson†	11,005	$18,357§	53	B
7.	Suffolk†	52,141	$15,751	51	B
8.	Williamsburg†	11,530	$15,429§	31	C–
9.	Newport News†	170,045	$15,721	28	D
10.	Hampton†	133,793	$14,460	27	D
11.	Norfolk†*	261,229	$14,211	18	F
	Portsmouth†*	103,907	$14,448	18	F

*Tied in rank.
†Independent cities.
§The U.S. Bureau of Economic Analysis combines small independent cities with adjacent cities or counties for the purposes of calculating per capita income. James City County and Williamsburg formed a single unit for the income study, as did York County and Poquoson.
Entire metro area is in Virginia.

Biggest Cities

City	County	Median House Price	Population
Virginia Beach	(independent city)	$96,500	393,069
Norfolk	(independent city)	$74,500	261,229
Newport News	(independent city)	$85,200	170,045
Chesapeake	(independent city)	$88,200	151,976
Hampton	(independent city)	$78,200	133,793
Portsmouth	(independent city)	$67,400	103,907
Suffolk	(independent city)	$70,700	52,141

Annual Unemployment Rates

Year	Metro Area	National
1985	5.1%	7.2%
1986	4.9%	7.0%
1987	4.7%	6.2%
1988	4.5%	5.5%
1989	4.6%	5.3%
1990	4.7%	5.5%

Major Employment Sectors

Sector	Jobs	Market Share	Average Pay	5-Year Trend
Services	150,600	26%	$17,399	Hot
Wholesale and retail trade	142,900	24%	$10,484	Hot
Government	136,800	23%	$24,161	Cool
Manufacturing	66,400	11%	$25,717	Cool
Construction	35,200	6%	$20,536	Cold
Transportation and utilities	27,700	5%	n.a.	Warm
Finance, insurance, and real estate	26,900	5%	$21,538	Warm

OKLAHOMA CITY

Total Points: 523
Overall Grade: C+
National Rank: 30 of 73
Regional Rank: 16 of 28 (South)

Metro Area Report Card

Category	Points	Grade
Economic Momentum	14	F
Future Growth	60	C+
Job Opportunities	33	D
Business Opportunities	58	B
Real Estate Opportunities	91	A
Equality of Opportunities	58	B
Overall	523	C+

Growth Potential of Metro Area Counties

Rank	County	Population	Per Capita Income	Growth Potential Points	Grade
1.	Cleveland	174,253	$14,307	49	B
2.	Canadian	74,409	$14,491	37	C
3.	McClain*	22,795	$12,763	29	D+
	Oklahoma*	599,611	$16,490	29	D+
5.	Pottawatomie	58,760	$13,021	26	D
6.	Logan	29,011	$12,555	24	D

*Tied in rank.
Entire metro area is in Oklahoma.

Biggest Cities

City	County	Median House Price	Population
Oklahoma City	Oklahoma	$54,900	444,719
Norman	Cleveland	$65,600	80,071
Edmond	Oklahoma	$80,000	52,315
Midwest City	Oklahoma	$48,300	52,267
Moore	Cleveland	$51,200	40,318
Shawnee	Pottawatomie	$40,200	26,017
Del City	Oklahoma	$43,300	23,928
Yukon	Canadian	$56,800	20,935
Bethany	Oklahoma	$53,600	20,075

Annual Unemployment Rates

Year	Metro Area	National
1985	5.9%	7.2%
1986	6.7%	7.0%
1987	6.0%	6.2%
1988	5.5%	5.5%
1989	4.6%	5.3%
1990	5.4%	5.5%

Major Employment Sectors

Sector	Jobs	Market Share	Average Pay	5-Year Trend
Services	106,100	25%	$18,356	Hot
Wholesale and retail trade	103,200	24%	$11,395	Cold
Government	102,000	24%	$22,468	Cold
Manufacturing	47,800	11%	$26,990	Cold
Finance, insurance, and real estate	24,500	6%	$21,793	Cold
Transportation and utilities	21,200	5%	n.a.	Cold
Construction	12,000	3%	$21,273	Cold

OMAHA

Total Points: 506
Overall Grade: C
National Rank: 38 of 73
Regional Rank: 5 of 14 (Midwest)

Metro Area Report Card

Category	Points	Grade
Economic Momentum	25	D–
Future Growth	65	B
Job Opportunities	60	B–
Business Opportunities	55	B–
Real Estate Opportunities	69	C
Equality of Opportunities	33	C
Overall	506	C

Growth Potential of Metro Area Counties

Rank	County	Population	Per Capita Income	Growth Potential Points	Grade
1.	Sarpy	102,583	$15,009	49	B
2.	Washington	16,607	$15,686	34	C
3.	Douglas	416,444	$17,674	29	D+
4.	Pottawattamie, Iowa	82,628	$14,509	24	D

Counties are in Nebraska unless otherwise indicated.

Biggest Cities

City	County	Median House Price	Population
Omaha	Douglas	$54,600	335,795
Council Bluffs, Iowa	Pottawattamie	$44,500	54,315
Bellevue	Sarpy	$62,100	30,982

Cities are in Nebraska unless otherwise indicated.

Annual Unemployment Rates

Year	Metro Area	National
1985	5.8%	7.2%
1986	5.3%	7.0%
1987	5.2%	6.2%
1988	3.9%	5.5%
1989	3.4%	5.3%
1990	2.6%	5.5%

Major Employment Sectors

Sector	Jobs	Market Share	Average Pay	5-Year Trend
Services	98,800	30%	$17,152	Hot
Wholesale and retail trade	82,100	25%	$10,614	Warm
Government	47,400	14%	$22,481	Cool
Manufacturing	36,800	11%	$25,059	Hot
Finance, insurance, and real estate	28,700	9%	$23,399	Cold
Transportation and utilities	23,500	7%	n.a.	Cold
Construction	12,800	4%	$23,373	Cold

_...

'°_, stop.

ORLANDO

Total Points: 747
Overall Grade: A
National Rank: 2 of 73
Regional Rank: 2 of 28 (South)

Metro Area Report Card

Category	Points	Grade
Economic Momentum	80	A
Future Growth	76	B+
Job Opportunities	88	A+
Business Opportunities	64	B+
Real Estate Opportunities	72	C+
Equality of Opportunities	36	C+
Overall	747	A

Growth Potential of Metro Area Counties

Rank	County	Population	Per Capita Income	Growth Potential Points	Grade
1.	Osceola	107,728	$17,596	76	A
2.	Seminole	287,529	$16,316	70	A
3.	Orange	677,491	$18,083	63	A

Entire metro area is in Florida.

Biggest Cities

City	County	Median House Price	Population
Orlando	Orange	$74,300	164,693
Pine Hills*	Orange	$68,500	35,322
Altamonte Springs	Seminole	$90,000	34,879
Sanford	Seminole	$59,300	32,387
Kissimmee	Osceola	$74,400	30,050
Wekiva Springs*	Seminole	$147,400	23,026
Winter Park	Orange	$138,600	22,242
Winter Springs	Seminole	$96,500	22,151

*Census Designated Places. All others are incorporated communities.

Annual Unemployment Rates

Year	Metro Area	National
1985	4.9%	7.2%
1986	4.6%	7.0%
1987	4.6%	6.2%
1988	4.5%	5.5%
1989	5.0%	5.3%
1990	5.3%	5.5%

Major Employment Sectors

Sector	Jobs	Market Share	Average Pay	5-Year Trend
Services	202,000	36%	$19,526	Hot
Wholesale and retail trade	148,100	26%	$12,472	Hot
Government	65,100	11%	$22,241	Hot
Manufacturing	54,100	10%	$28,413	Hot
Construction	37,100	7%	$21,771	Warm
Finance, insurance, and real estate	32,600	6%	$24,981	Hot
Transportation and utilities	29,400	5%	n.a.	Hot

PHILADELPHIA

Total Points: 436
Overall Grade: C–
National Rank: 55 of 73
Regional Rank: 10 of 17 (East)

Metro Area Report Card

Category	Points	Grade
Economic Momentum	51	C+
Future Growth	35	D
Job Opportunities	52	C
Business Opportunities	44	C
Real Estate Opportunities	63	C
Equality of Opportunities	17	C–
Overall	436	C–

Growth Potential of Metro Area Counties

Rank	County	Population	Per Capita Income	Growth Potential Points	Grade
1.	Chester	376,396	$22,491	54	B
2.	Burlington, N.J.	395,066	$21,270	48	B
3.	Gloucester, N.J.	230,082	$18,187	47	B
4.	Cecil, Md.	71,347	$16,768	46	B–
5.	Bucks	541,174	$20,534	45	B–
6.	Cumberland, N.J.	138,053	$15,869	41	C
7.	New Castle, Del.	441,946	$20,907	39	C
8.	Mercer, N.J.	325,824	$23,913	37	C
9.	Montgomery*	678,111	$25,989	34	C
	Salem, N.J.*	65,294	$16,933	34	C
11.	Camden, N.J.	502,824	$19,180	26	D
12.	Delaware	547,651	$21,991	22	D–
13.	Philadelphia	1,585,577	$15,479	18	F

*Tied in rank.
Counties are in Pennsylvania unless otherwise indicated.

Biggest Cities

City	County	Median House Price	Population
Philadelphia	Philadelphia	$49,400	1,585,577
Trenton, N.J.	Mercer	$71,300	88,675
Camden, N.J.	Camden	$31,300	87,492
Wilmington, Del.	New Castle	$77,800	71,529
Cherry Hill, N.J.*	Camden	$149,700	69,319
Levittown*	Bucks	$103,700	55,362
Vineland, N.J.	Cumberland	$83,600	54,780
Chester	Delaware	$38,400	41,856
Willingboro, N.J.*	Burlington	$95,800	36,291
Pennsauken, N.J.*	Camden	$91,000	34,733

*Census Designated Places. All others are incorporated communities.
Cities are in Pennsylvania unless otherwise indicated.

Annual Unemployment Rates

Year	Metro Area	National
1985	5.9%	7.2%
1986	5.2%	7.0%
1987	4.4%	6.2%
1988	4.1%	5.5%
1989	3.8%	5.3%
1990	4.8%	5.5%

Major Employment Sectors

Sector	Jobs	Market Share	Average Pay	5-Year Trend
Services	842,300	30%	$23,067	Hot
Wholesale and retail trade	612,600	22%	$13,197	Cool
Manufacturing	452,300	16%	$32,361	Cold
Government	411,200	15%	$26,988	Cold
Finance, insurance, and real estate	206,100	7%	$28,590	Hot
Transportation and utilities	126,800	5%	n.a.	Warm
Construction	124,300	4%	$29,110	Hot

PHOENIX

Total Points: 638
Overall Grade: A–
National Rank: 7 of 73
Regional Rank: 4 of 14 (West)

Metro Area Report Card

Category	Points	Grade
Economic Momentum	62	B+
Future Growth	91	A
Job Opportunities	61	B
Business Opportunities	42	C
Real Estate Opportunities	73	C+
Equality of Opportunities	35	C+
Overall	638	A–

Growth Potential of Metro Area County

County	Population	Per Capita Income	Growth Potential Points	Grade
Maricopa	2,122,101	$17,705	56	B+

Entire metro area is in Arizona.

Biggest Cities

City	County	Median House Price	Population
Phoenix	Maricopa	$77,100	983,403
Mesa	Maricopa	$86,500	288,091
Glendale	Maricopa	$84,900	148,134
Tempe	Maricopa	$91,500	141,865
Scottsdale	Maricopa	$115,200	130,069
Chandler	Maricopa	$90,300	90,533
Peoria	Maricopa	$85,500	50,618
Sun City*	Maricopa	$73,000	38,126
Gilbert	Maricopa	$108,500	29,188

*Census Designated Place. All others are incorporated communities.

Annual Unemployment Rates

Year	Metro Area	National
1985	5.1%	7.2%
1986	5.6%	7.0%
1987	5.2%	6.2%
1988	5.1%	5.5%
1989	4.3%	5.3%
1990	4.3%	5.5%

Major Employment Sectors

Sector	Jobs	Market Share	Average Pay	5-Year Trend
Services	275,900	28%	$20,241	Hot
Wholesale and retail trade	248,200	25%	$12,922	Hot
Manufacturing	138,200	14%	$28,959	Warm
Government	133,300	14%	$24,787	Hot
Finance, insurance, and real estate	75,400	8%	$25,926	Hot
Transportation and utilities	58,400	6%	n.a.	Hot
Construction	55,500	6%	$22,737	Cold

PITTSBURGH

Total Points: 423
Overall Grade: D+
National Rank: 59 of 73
Regional Rank: 13 of 17 (East)

Metro Area Report Card

Category	Points	Grade
Economic Momentum	34	C–
Future Growth	44	C–
Job Opportunities	36	D
Business Opportunities	49	C
Real Estate Opportunities	77	B–
Equality of Opportunities	16	D+
Overall	423	D+

Growth Potential of Metro Area Counties

Rank	County	Population	Per Capita Income	Growth Potential Points	Grade
1.	Westmoreland	370,321	$15,681	32	C–
2.	Washington	204,584	$15,436	28	D
3.	Beaver	186,093	$14,046	26	D
4.	Fayette	145,351	$12,930	24	D
5.	Allegheny	1,336,449	$19,249	20	F

Entire metro area is in Pennsylvania.

270 ## Biggest Cities

City	County	Median House Price	Population
Pittsburgh	Allegheny	$41,200	369,879
Penn Hills*	Allegheny	$53,200	51,430
Bethel Park	Allegheny	$82,200	33,823
Ross Township*	Allegheny	$74,600	33,482
Mount Lebanon*	Allegheny	$103,600	33,362
Shaler Township*	Allegheny	$71,200	30,533
Monroeville	Allegheny	$66,700	29,169
McCandless Township*	Allegheny	$102,000	28,781
McKeesport	Allegheny	$27,800	26,016
Plum	Allegheny	$63,700	25,609

*Census Designated Places. All others are incorporated communities.

Annual Unemployment Rates

Year	Metro Area	National
1985	9.8%	7.2%
1986	8.3%	7.0%
1987	6.9%	6.2%
1988	6.0%	5.5%
1989	4.7%	5.3%
1990	5.0%	5.5%

Major Employment Sectors

Sector	Jobs	Market Share	Average Pay	5-Year Trend
Services	323,300	33%	$21,253	Hot
Wholesale and retail trade	237,300	24%	$10,881	Cool
Manufacturing	128,700	13%	$31,403	Cold
Government	114,300	12%	$24,476	Cold
Transportation and utilities	59,400	6%	n.a.	Hot
Finance, insurance, and real estate	57,000	6%	$25,834	Cool
Construction	46,100	5%	$26,456	Cool

PORTLAND

Total Points: 597
Overall Grade: B
National Rank: 15 of 73
Regional Rank: 7 of 14 (West)

Metro Area Report Card

Category	Points	Grade
Economic Momentum	46	C
Future Growth	65	B
Job Opportunities	64	B
Business Opportunities	57	B
Real Estate Opportunities	56	C–
Equality of Opportunities	66	A–
Overall	597	B

Growth Potential of Metro Area Counties

Rank	County	Population	Per Capita Income	Growth Potential Points	Grade
1.	Clark, Wash.*	238,053	$15,379	49	B
	Washington*	311,554	$18,191	49	B
3.	Clackamas*	278,850	$18,596	37	C
	Yamhill*	65,551	$14,585	37	C
5.	Multnomah	583,887	$18,308	24	D

*Tied in rank.
Counties are in Oregon unless otherwise indicated.

Biggest Cities   **273**

City	County	Median House Price	Population
Portland	Multnomah	$59,200	437,319
Gresham	Multnomah	$71,100	68,235
Beaverton	Washington	$89,800	53,310
Vancouver, Wash.	Clark	$61,300	46,380
Hillsboro	Washington	$71,900	37,520
Aloha*	Washington	$71,800	34,284
Lake Oswego	Clackamas	$142,600	30,576
Tigard	Washington	$90,400	29,344
Powellhurst-Centennial*	Multnomah	$56,900	28,756

*Census Designated Places. All others are incorporated communities.
Cities are in Oregon unless otherwise indicated.

Annual Unemployment Rates

Year	Metro Area	National
1985	7.4%	7.2%
1986	7.2%	7.0%
1987	5.3%	6.2%
1988	4.8%	5.5%
1989	4.5%	5.3%
1990	4.2%	5.5%

Unemployment statistics for Clark County, Wash., were not available from the U.S. Bureau of Labor Statistics. The above figures are for the remainder of the metro area.

Major Employment Sectors

Sector	Jobs	Market Share	Average Pay	5-Year Trend
Services	165,500	26%	$19,169	Hot
Wholesale and retail trade	164,800	26%	$12,648	Hot
Manufacturing	104,100	16%	$27,888	Hot
Government	83,900	13%	$24,676	Warm
Finance, insurance, and real estate	51,200	8%	$24,602	Hot
Transportation and utilities	37,600	6%	n.a.	Warm
Construction	29,400	5%	$25,338	Hot

Statistics for Clark County, Wash., were not available from the U.S. Bureau of Labor Statistics. The above figures are for the remainder of the metro area.

PROVIDENCE

Total Points: 420
Overall Grade: D
National Rank: 61 of 73
Regional Rank: 15 of 17 (East)

Metro Area Report Card

Category	Points	Grade
Economic Momentum	45	C
Future Growth	38	D
Job Opportunities	50	C
Business Opportunities	65	B+
Real Estate Opportunities	40	D
Equality of Opportunities	14	D
Overall	420	D

Growth Potential of Metro Area Counties

Rank	County	Population	Per Capita Income	Growth Potential Points	Grade
1.	Washington	110,006	$19,142	54	B
2.	Kent	161,135	$19,300	39	C
3.	Bristol*	48,859	$20,663	33	C
	Providence*	596,270	$17,117	33	C

*Tied in rank.
Entire metro area is in Rhode Island.

Biggest Cities

City	County	Median House Price	Population
Providence	Providence	$113,000	160,728
Warwick	Kent	$116,600	85,427
Cranston	Providence	$129,700	76,060
Pawtucket	Providence	$112,500	72,644
East Providence	Providence	$122,500	50,380
Woonsocket	Providence	$118,800	43,877
North Providence*	Providence	$129,200	32,090
West Warwick*	Kent	$123,300	29,268
Bristol*	Bristol	$151,500	21,625

*Census Designated Places. All others are incorporated communities.

Annual Unemployment Rates

Year	Metro Area	National
1985	4.9%	7.2%
1986	4.0%	7.0%
1987	3.7%	6.2%
1988	2.9%	5.5%
1989	3.8%	5.3%
1990	6.5%	5.5%

The U.S. Bureau of Labor Statistics calculates the unemployment rate for a geographic area that is slightly different from the Providence metro area defined by this book. Selected towns in the outer portion of the metro area are not included in the above statistics.

Major Employment Sectors

Sector	Jobs	Market Share	Average Pay	5-Year Trend
Services	96,300	30%	$19,401	Hot
Wholesale and retail trade	65,700	21%	$12,460	Cold
Manufacturing	62,800	20%	$22,562	Cold
Government	46,400	15%	$26,519	Cool
Finance, insurance, and real estate	22,400	7%	$27,257	Cool
Construction	13,600	4%	$26,228	Hot
Transportation and utilities	12,000	4%	n.a.	Hot

All figures are for the modified metro area used by the U.S. Bureau of Labor Statistics in its calculations.

RALEIGH

Total Points: 692
Overall Grade: A
National Rank: 4 of 73
Regional Rank: 3 of 28 (South)

Metro Area Report Card

Category	Points	Grade
Economic Momentum	69	A
Future Growth	57	C
Job Opportunities	80	A
Business Opportunities	70	A
Real Estate Opportunities	71	C
Equality of Opportunities	39	B–
Overall	692	A

Growth Potential of Metro Area Counties

Rank	County	Population	Per Capita Income	Growth Potential Points	Grade
1.	Wake	423,380	$20,025	66	A
2.	Orange	93,851	$18,295	56	B+
3.	Durham	181,835	$18,346	53	B
4.	Franklin	36,414	$11,563	43	C+

Entire metro area is in North Carolina.

Biggest Cities

City	County	Median House Price	Population
Raleigh	Wake	$96,600	207,951
Durham	Durham	$80,600	136,611
Cary	Wake	$108,800	43,858
Chapel Hill	Orange	$141,100	38,719

Annual Unemployment Rates

Year	Metro Area	National
1985	2.8%	7.2%
1986	3.3%	7.0%
1987	3.1%	6.2%
1988	2.6%	5.5%
1989	2.4%	5.3%
1990	2.5%	5.5%

Major Employment Sectors

Sector	Jobs	Market Share	Average Pay	5-Year Trend
Services	114,700	27%	$20,192	Hot
Government	94,800	22%	$24,497	Warm
Wholesale and retail trade	90,500	21%	$11,449	Hot
Manufacturing	63,800	15%	$30,578	Hot
Finance, insurance, and real estate	24,400	6%	$23,146	Hot
Construction	22,300	5%	$19,927	Cold
Transportation and utilities	21,500	5%	n.a.	Hot

RICHMOND

Total Points: 578
Overall Grade: B
National Rank: 19 of 73
Regional Rank: 10 of 28 (South)

Metro Area Report Card

Category	Points	Grade
Economic Momentum	56	B–
Future Growth	69	B
Job Opportunities	68	B
Business Opportunities	51	C+
Real Estate Opportunities	76	C+
Equality of Opportunities	20	C
Overall	578	B

Growth Potential of Metro Area Counties

Rank County	Population	Per Capita Income	Growth Potential Points	Grade
1. Chesterfield	209,274	$20,696	70	A
2. Hanover	63,306	$20,532	56	B+
3. Powhatan	15,328	$16,739	55	B
4. Goochland	14,163	$21,973	53	B
5. Henrico	217,881	$23,353	52	B
6. New Kent	10,445	$17,444	42	C+
7. Prince George	27,394	$12,673§	39	C
8. Charles City	6,282	$16,374	35	C
9. Dinwiddie	20,960	$14,211§	34	C
10. Petersburg†	38,386	$14,211§	24	D
11. Colonial Heights†	16,064	$14,211§	23	D
12. Richmond†	203,056	$20,852	20	F
13. Hopewell†	23,101	$12,673§	17	F

†Independent cities.
§The U.S. Bureau of Economic Analysis combines small independent cities with adjacent cities or counties for the purposes of calculating per capita income. Prince George County and Hopewell formed a single unit for the income study, as did Dinwiddie County, Colonial Heights, and Petersburg.
Entire metro area is in Virginia.

Biggest Cities

City	County	Median House Price	Population
Richmond	(independent city)	$66,600	203,056
Tuckahoe*	Henrico	$110,100	42,629
Petersburg	(independent city)	$52,000	38,386
Hopewell	(independent city)	$54,300	23,101
Mechanicsville*	Hanover	$89,500	22,027

*Census Designated Places. All others are incorporated communities.

Annual Unemployment Rates

Year	Metro Area	National
1985	4.8%	7.2%
1986	4.4%	7.0%
1987	3.7%	6.2%
1988	3.4%	5.5%
1989	3.6%	5.3%
1990	3.9%	5.5%

Major Employment Sectors

Sector	Jobs	Market Share	Average Pay	5-Year Trend
Services	109,500	23%	$18,166	Hot
Wholesale and retail trade	108,600	23%	$12,901	Warm
Government	97,400	20%	$23,576	Cool
Manufacturing	64,900	14%	$31,758	Warm
Finance, insurance, and real estate	40,200	8%	$27,115	Hot
Construction	31,000	7%	$22,502	Hot
Transportation and utilities	23,900	5%	n.a.	Warm

ROCHESTER

Total Points: 423
Overall Grade: D+
National Rank: 59 of 73
Regional Rank: 13 of 17 (East)

Metro Area Report Card

Category	Points	Grade
Economic Momentum	48	C
Future Growth	45	C–
Job Opportunities	52	C
Business Opportunities	28	D–
Real Estate Opportunities	58	C
Equality of Opportunities	20	C
Overall	423	D+

Growth Potential of Metro Area Counties

Rank	County	Population	Per Capita Income	Growth Potential Points	Growth Potential Grade
1.	Livingston	62,372	$15,772	35	C
2.	Ontario	95,101	$17,869	34	C
3.	Orleans*	41,846	$15,213	32	C–
	Wayne*	89,123	$16,296	32	C–
5.	Monroe	713,968	$21,192	30	C–

*Tied in rank.
Entire metro area is in New York.

Biggest Cities

City	County	Median House Price	Population
Rochester	Monroe	$65,200	231,636
Irondequoit*	Monroe	$89,700	52,322
Brighton*	Monroe	$117,000	34,455

*Census Designated Places. All others are incorporated communities.

Annual Unemployment Rates

Year	Metro Area	National
1985	5.2%	7.2%
1986	5.7%	7.0%
1987	4.4%	6.2%
1988	3.8%	5.5%
1989	4.2%	5.3%
1990	3.7%	5.5%

Major Employment Sectors

Sector	Jobs	Market Share	Average Pay	5-Year Trend
Manufacturing	133,300	27%	$35,816	Cold
Services	125,400	26%	$18,441	Hot
Wholesale and retail trade	104,900	21%	$11,313	Warm
Government	68,300	14%	$25,738	Cool
Finance, insurance, and real estate	23,300	5%	$25,532	Hot
Construction	19,200	4%	$26,560	Hot
Transportation and utilities	15,200	3%	n.a.	Warm

SACRAMENTO

Total Points: 655
Overall Grade: A–
National Rank: 6 of 73
Regional Rank: 3 of 14 (West)

Metro Area Report Card

Category	Points	Grade
Economic Momentum	71	A
Future Growth	80	A
Job Opportunities	70	B+
Business Opportunities	34	C–
Real Estate Opportunities	57	C
Equality of Opportunities	51	B
Overall	655	A–

Growth Potential of Metro Area Counties

Rank	County	Population	Per Capita Income	Growth Potential Points	Grade
1.	Placer	172,796	$19,337	56	B+
2.	El Dorado	125,995	$17,264	54	B
3.	Sacramento	1,041,219	$18,194	46	B–
4.	Yolo	141,092	$18,816	42	C+

Entire metro area is in California.

Biggest Cities

City	County	Median House Price	Population
Sacramento	Sacramento	$115,800	369,365
Citrus Heights*	Sacramento	$131,600	107,439
Arden-Arcade*	Sacramento	$151,000	92,040
Rancho Cordova*	Sacramento	$111,700	48,731
Carmichael*	Sacramento	$161,000	48,702
Davis	Yolo	$191,300	46,209
Roseville	Placer	$158,500	44,685
North Highlands*	Sacramento	$89,400	42,105
Woodland	Yolo	$131,300	39,802
Parkway-South Sacramento*	Sacramento	$83,300	31,903

*Census Designated Places. All others are incorporated communities.

Annual Unemployment Rates

Year	Metro Area	National
1985	7.1%	7.2%
1986	6.2%	7.0%
1987	5.6%	6.2%
1988	5.4%	5.5%
1989	4.9%	5.3%
1990	4.8%	5.5%

Major Employment Sectors **287**

Sector	Jobs	Market Share	Average Pay	5-Year Trend
Government	185,000	29%	$28,082	Hot
Wholesale and retail trade	145,700	23%	$13,106	Hot
Services	142,300	23%	$20,539	Hot
Manufacturing	45,600	7%	$27,801	Hot
Finance, insurance, and real estate	41,100	7%	$23,860	Hot
Construction	40,700	6%	$26,587	Hot
Transportation and utilities	28,500	5%	n.a.	Hot

SAINT LOUIS

Total Points: 489
Overall Grade: C
National Rank: 43 of 73
Regional Rank: 6 of 14 (Midwest)

Metro Area Report Card

Category	Points	Grade
Economic Momentum	36	C–
Future Growth	52	C
Job Opportunities	44	C
Business Opportunities	48	C
Real Estate Opportunities	84	B+
Equality of Opportunities	29	C
Overall	489	C

Growth Potential of Metro Area Counties

Rank County	Population	Per Capita Income	Growth Potential Points	Grade
1. Saint Charles	212,907	$17,361	66	A
2. Jefferson	171,380	$14,818	43	C+
3. Franklin	80,603	$15,776	35	C
4. Saint Clair, Ill.	262,852	$15,097	33	C
5. Madison, Ill.	249,238	$16,858	32	C–
6. Monroe, Ill.	22,422	$18,742	30	C–
7. Clinton, Ill.	33,944	$15,899	27	D
8. Jersey, Ill.*	20,539	$14,172	24	D
Saint Louis County*	993,529	$22,598	24	D
10. Saint Louis city†	396,685	$17,513	17	F

*Tied in rank.
†Independent city.
Counties are in Missouri unless otherwise indicated.

Biggest Cities

City	County	Median House Price	Population
Saint Louis	(independent city)	$50,700	396,685
Saint Charles	Saint Charles	$80,700	54,555
Florissant	Saint Louis	$67,200	51,206
Saint Peters	Saint Charles	$86,000	45,779
Belleville, Ill.	Saint Clair	$58,500	42,785
East Saint Louis, Ill.	Saint Clair	$26,400	40,944
University City	Saint Louis	$75,200	40,087
Chesterfield	Saint Louis	$172,800	37,991
Alton, Ill.	Madison	$37,500	32,905
Granite City, Ill.	Madison	$42,700	32,862

Cities are in Missouri unless otherwise indicated.

Annual Unemployment Rates

Year	Metro Area	National
1985	7.4%	7.2%
1986	7.0%	7.0%
1987	6.6%	6.2%
1988	6.0%	5.5%
1989	5.5%	5.3%
1990	5.9%	5.5%

290   Major Employment Sectors

Sector	Jobs	Market Share	Average Pay	5-Year Trend
Services	323,700	27%	$19,819	Hot
Wholesale and retail trade	282,600	24%	$11,961	Warm
Manufacturing	223,000	19%	$32,478	Cool
Government	143,500	12%	$23,695	Cold
Transportation and utilities	78,100	7%	n.a.	Cool
Finance, insurance, and real estate	76,500	6%	$25,878	Warm
Construction	56,800	5%	$27,965	Cool

SALT LAKE CITY

Total Points: 484
Overall Grade: C
National Rank: 45 of 73
Regional Rank: 12 of 14 (West)

Metro Area Report Card

Category	Points	Grade
Economic Momentum	39	C
Future Growth	61	C+
Job Opportunities	56	C+
Business Opportunities	17	F
Real Estate Opportunities	72	C+
Equality of Opportunities	44	B
Overall	484	C

Growth Potential of Metro Area Counties

Rank	County	Population	Per Capita Income	Growth Potential Points	Growth Potential Grade
1.	Davis	187,941	$12,430	46	B–
2.	Weber	158,330	$14,148	36	C
3.	Salt Lake	725,956	$14,315	35	C

Entire metro area is in Utah.

292

Biggest Cities

City	County	Median House Price	Population
Salt Lake City	Salt Lake	$67,200	159,936
West Valley City	Salt Lake	$58,300	86,976
Sandy	Salt Lake	$87,500	75,058
Ogden	Weber	$54,700	63,909
Taylorsville-Bennion*	Salt Lake	$66,900	52,351
West Jordan	Salt Lake	$67,600	42,892
Layton	Davis	$72,700	41,784
Bountiful	Davis	$87,100	36,659
Millcreek*	Salt Lake	$69,900	32,230
Murray	Salt Lake	$74,900	31,282

*Census Designated Places. All others are incorporated communities.

Annual Unemployment Rates

Year	Metro Area	National
1985	5.3%	7.2%
1986	5.3%	7.0%
1987	5.7%	6.2%
1988	4.6%	5.5%
1989	4.5%	5.3%
1990	4.1%	5.5%

Major Employment Sectors

Sector	Jobs	Market Share	Average Pay	5-Year Trend
Services	122,000	25%	$17,695	Hot
Wholesale and retail trade	121,400	25%	$11,263	Warm
Government	98,600	20%	$22,143	Cool
Manufacturing	69,000	14%	$24,269	Hot
Transportation and utilities	32,800	7%	n.a.	Hot
Finance, insurance, and real estate	27,900	6%	$22,064	Cold
Construction	19,200	4%	$22,177	Cold

SAN ANTONIO

Total Points: 447
Overall Grade: C–
National Rank: 52 of 73
Regional Rank: 23 of 28 (South)

Metro Area Report Card

Category	Points	Grade
Economic Momentum	29	D
Future Growth	57	C
Job Opportunities	35	D
Business Opportunities	29	D
Real Estate Opportunities	79	B
Equality of Opportunities	40	B–
Overall	447	C–

Growth Potential of Metro Area Counties

Rank	County	Population	Per Capita Income	Growth Potential Points	Grade
1.	Guadalupe	64,873	$13,838	46	B–
2.	Comal	51,832	$16,653	44	C+
3.	Bexar	1,185,394	$14,053	37	C

Entire metro area is in Texas.

Biggest Cities

City	County	Median House Price	Population
San Antonio	Bexar	$49,700	935,933
New Braunfels	Comal	$65,500	27,334
Seguin	Guadalupe	$45,700	18,853

Annual Unemployment Rates

Year	Metro Area	National
1985	6.0%	7.2%
1986	7.3%	7.0%
1987	7.9%	6.2%
1988	7.8%	5.5%
1989	7.3%	5.3%
1990	6.9%	5.5%

Major Employment Sectors

Sector	Jobs	Market Share	Average Pay	5-Year Trend
Services	140,400	27%	$17,899	Hot
Wholesale and retail trade	130,300	25%	$11,956	Cool
Government	120,100	23%	$24,850	Warm
Manufacturing	44,500	9%	$21,461	Cold
Finance, insurance, and real estate	39,800	8%	$23,088	Cool
Transportation and utilities	21,900	4%	n.a.	Hot
Construction	21,700	4%	$19,156	Cold

SAN DIEGO

Total Points: 603
Overall Grade: B
National Rank: 13 of 73
Regional Rank: 6 of 14 (West)

Metro Area Report Card

Category	Points	Grade
Economic Momentum	64	A–
Future Growth	73	B+
Job Opportunities	75	A
Business Opportunities	32	D+
Real Estate Opportunities	39	D
Equality of Opportunities	53	B
Overall	603	B

Growth Potential of Metro Area County

County	Population	Per Capita Income	Growth Potential Points	Grade
San Diego	2,498,016	$18,651	54	B

Entire metro area is in California.

Biggest Cities

City	County	Median House Price	Population
San Diego	San Diego	$189,400	1,110,549
Chula Vista	San Diego	$164,000	135,163
Oceanside	San Diego	$170,200	128,398
Escondido	San Diego	$169,500	108,635
El Cajon	San Diego	$158,000	88,693
Vista	San Diego	$183,400	71,872
Carlsbad	San Diego	$255,900	63,126
Encinitas	San Diego	$285,700	55,386
Spring Valley*	San Diego	$142,900	55,331
National City	San Diego	$114,700	54,249

*Census Designated Place. All others are incorporated communities.

Annual Unemployment Rates

Year	Metro Area	National
1985	5.3%	7.2%
1986	5.0%	7.0%
1987	4.5%	6.2%
1988	4.3%	5.5%
1989	3.9%	5.3%
1990	4.5%	5.5%

298

Major Employment Sectors

Sector	Jobs	Market Share	Average Pay	5-Year Trend
Services	275,700	28%	$21,606	Hot
Wholesale and retail trade	238,100	24%	$13,201	Hot
Government	176,800	18%	$25,744	Hot
Manufacturing	136,500	14%	$29,966	Hot
Finance, insurance, and real estate	67,900	7%	$27,602	Hot
Construction	62,300	6%	$26,924	Hot
Transportation and utilities	37,100	4%	n.a.	Hot

SAN FRANCISCO

Total Points: 584
Overall Grade: B
National Rank: 18 of 73
Regional Rank: 8 of 14 (West)

Metro Area Report Card

Category	Points	Grade
Economic Momentum	51	C+
Future Growth	47	C–
Job Opportunities	54	C
Business Opportunities	66	A–
Real Estate Opportunities	27	F
Equality of Opportunities	88	A+
Overall	584	B

Growth Potential of Metro Area Counties

Rank	County	Population	Per Capita Income	Growth Potential Points	Grade
1.	Solano	340,421	$16,154	60	A–
2.	Sonoma	388,222	$20,860	52	B
3.	Santa Cruz	229,734	$18,637	48	B
4.	Marin	230,096	$34,983	44	C+
5.	Contra Costa	803,732	$24,308	43	C+
6.	Santa Clara	1,497,577	$24,581	41	C
7.	Napa	110,765	$21,417	37	C
8.	San Mateo	649,623	$27,659	33	C
9.	Alameda	1,279,182	$20,967	31	C–
10.	San Francisco	723,959	$26,454	21	D–

Entire metro area is in California.

Biggest Cities

City	County	Median House Price	Population
San Jose	Santa Clara	$259,100	782,248
San Francisco	San Francisco	$298,900	723,959
Oakland	Alameda	$177,400	372,242
Fremont	Alameda	$264,300	173,339
Sunnyvale	Santa Clara	$332,700	117,229
Santa Rosa	Sonoma	$193,800	113,313
Hayward	Alameda	$184,500	111,498
Concord	Contra Costa	$195,300	111,348
Vallejo	Solano	$140,600	109,199
Berkeley	Alameda	$261,000	102,724

Annual Unemployment Rates

Year	Metro Area	National
1985	5.8%	7.2%
1986	5.5%	7.0%
1987	4.6%	6.2%
1988	4.2%	5.5%
1989	3.9%	5.3%
1990	4.0%	5.5%

Unemployment statistics for Santa Cruz County were not available from the U.S. Bureau of Labor Statistics. The above figures are for the remainder of the metro area.

Major Employment Sectors   **301**

Sector	Jobs	Market Share	Average Pay	5-Year Trend
Services	832,500	28%	$24,766	Hot
Wholesale and retail trade	676,400	23%	$15,306	Warm
Manufacturing	492,100	16%	$36,208	Cool
Government	457,800	15%	$28,802	Cool
Finance, insurance, and real estate	213,100	7%	$33,114	Cold
Transportation and utilities	174,400	6%	n.a.	Cool
Construction	145,500	5%	$32,204	Hot

Statistics for Santa Cruz County were not available from the U.S. Bureau of Labor Statistics. The above figures are for the remainder of the metro area.

SCRANTON

Total Points: 522
Overall Grade: C+
National Rank: 31 of 73
Regional Rank: 2 of 17 (East)

Metro Area Report Card

Category	Points	Grade
Economic Momentum	47	C
Future Growth	57	C
Job Opportunities	40	C–
Business Opportunities	52	C+
Real Estate Opportunities	82	B
Equality of Opportunities	35	C+
Overall	522	C+

Growth Potential of Metro Area Counties

Rank	County	Population	Per Capita Income	Growth Potential Points	Grade
1.	Monroe	95,709	$15,874	56	B+
2.	Luzerne	328,149	$15,423	37	C
3.	Lackawanna*	219,039	$16,003	36	C
	Wyoming*	28,076	$14,388	36	C
5.	Columbia	63,202	$14,230	33	C

*Tied in rank.
Entire metro area is in Pennsylvania.

Biggest Cities

City	County	Median House Price	Population
Scranton	Lackawanna	$57,100	81,805
Wilkes-Barre	Luzerne	$44,200	47,523
Hazleton	Luzerne	$43,900	24,730

Annual Unemployment Rates

Year	Metro Area	National
1985	9.5%	7.2%
1986	8.3%	7.0%
1987	6.9%	6.2%
1988	6.0%	5.5%
1989	5.5%	5.3%
1990	6.9%	5.5%

Major Employment Sectors

Sector	Jobs	Market Share	Average Pay	5-Year Trend
Services	78,400	25%	$16,344	Hot
Wholesale and retail trade	73,400	24%	$10,234	Hot
Manufacturing	69,400	23%	$20,666	Cold
Government	42,100	14%	$22,401	Cold
Transportation and utilities	16,700	5%	n.a.	Hot
Finance, insurance, and real estate	13,800	4%	$19,371	Hot
Construction	13,700	4%	$22,378	Hot

SEATTLE

Total Points: 677
Overall Grade: A
National Rank: 5 of 73
Regional Rank: 2 of 14 (West)

Metro Area Report Card

Category	Points	Grade
Economic Momentum	60	B
Future Growth	64	B–
Job Opportunities	76	A
Business Opportunities	57	B
Real Estate Opportunities	68	C
Equality of Opportunities	65	A–
Overall	677	A

Growth Potential of Metro Area Counties

Rank	County	Population	Per Capita Income	Growth Potential Points	Growth Potential Grade
1.	Snohomish	465,642	$17,832	50	B
2.	Pierce	586,203	$15,546	44	C+
3.	King	1,507,319	$22,125	43	C+

Entire metro area is in Washington.

Biggest Cities

City	County	Median House Price	Population
Seattle	King	$137,900	516,259
Tacoma	Pierce	$66,200	176,664
Bellevue	King	$192,800	86,874
Everett	Snohomish	$98,000	69,961
Federal Way*	King	$118,800	67,554
Lakewood*	Pierce	$88,300	58,412
East Hill-Meridian*	King	$126,600	42,696
Renton	King	$106,300	41,688
Kirkland	King	$160,200	40,052
Kent	King	$107,100	37,960

*Census Designated Places. All others are incorporated communities.

Annual Unemployment Rates

Year	Metro Area	National
1985	6.6%	7.2%
1986	6.5%	7.0%
1987	6.0%	6.2%
1988	4.8%	5.5%
1989	4.6%	5.3%
1990	3.5%	5.5%

Unemployment statistics for Pierce County were not available from the U.S. Bureau of Labor Statistics. The above figures are for the remainder of the metro area.

306   Major Employment Sectors

Sector	Jobs	Market Share	Average Pay	5-Year Trend
Services	272,900	25%	$19,068	Hot
Wholesale and retail trade	263,300	24%	$13,481	Hot
Manufacturing	222,600	20%	$32,118	Hot
Government	146,500	13%	$25,396	Hot
Finance, insurance, and real estate	74,000	7%	$26,394	Warm
Transportation and utilities	69,000	6%	n.a.	Hot
Construction	61,700	6%	$24,595	Hot

Statistics for Pierce County were not available from the U.S. Bureau of Labor Statistics. The above figures are for the remainder of the metro area.

SPRINGFIELD

Total Points: 466
Overall Grade: C
National Rank: 48 of 73
Regional Rank: 8 of 17 (East)

Metro Area Report Card

Category	Points	Grade
Economic Momentum	57	B
Future Growth	49	C
Job Opportunities	47	C
Business Opportunities	50	C
Real Estate Opportunities	57	C
Equality of Opportunities	15	D
Overall	466	C

Growth Potential of Metro Area Counties

Rank	County	Population	Per Capita Income	Growth Potential Points	Grade
1.	Hampshire	146,568	$17,619	48	B
2.	Hampden	456,310	$18,804	41	C

Entire metro area is in Massachusetts.

Biggest Cities

City	County	Median House Price	Population
Springfield	Hampden	$105,500	156,983
Chicopee	Hampden	$113,800	56,632
Holyoke	Hampden	$116,800	43,704
Westfield	Hampden	$136,000	38,372
Northampton	Hampshire	$132,900	29,289
West Springfield*	Hampden	$130,800	27,537

*Census Designated Place. All others are incorporated communities.

Annual Unemployment Rates

Year	Metro Area	National
1985	4.4%	7.2%
1986	4.2%	7.0%
1987	3.3%	6.2%
1988	3.3%	5.5%
1989	4.0%	5.3%
1990	5.8%	5.5%

The U.S. Bureau of Labor Statistics calculates the unemployment rate for a geographic area that is slightly different from the Springfield metro area defined by this book. Selected towns in the outer portion of the metro area are not included in the above statistics.

Major Employment Sectors

Sector	Jobs	Market Share	Average Pay	5-Year Trend
Services	62,600	27%	$19,686	Warm
Wholesale and retail trade	53,900	23%	$11,815	Cool
Manufacturing	46,100	20%	$27,102	Cold
Government	38,000	16%	$24,205	Cold
Finance, insurance, and real estate	15,400	7%	$25,546	Cold
Transportation and utilities	10,200	4%	n.a.	Hot
Construction	7,800	3%	$28,045	Cold

All figures are for the modified metro area used by the U.S. Bureau of Labor Statistics in its calculations.

SYRACUSE

Total Points: 430
Overall Grade: C–
National Rank: 56 of 73
Regional Rank: 11 of 17 (East)

Metro Area Report Card

Category	Points	Grade
Economic Momentum	43	C
Future Growth	51	C
Job Opportunities	47	C
Business Opportunities	44	C
Real Estate Opportunities	54	C–
Equality of Opportunities	16	D+
Overall	430	C–

Growth Potential of Metro Area Counties

Rank	County	Population	Per Capita Income	Growth Potential Points	Grade
1.	Onondaga	468,973	$18,794	38	C
2.	Madison	69,120	$15,232	34	C
3.	Oswego	121,771	$13,836	33	C

Entire metro area is in New York.

Biggest Cities

City	County	Median House Price	Population
Syracuse	Onondaga	$67,600	163,860
Oswego	Oswego	$58,500	19,195
Fulton	Oswego	$59,800	12,929

Annual Unemployment Rates

Year	Metro Area	National
1985	5.9%	7.2%
1986	7.4%	7.0%
1987	6.2%	6.2%
1988	4.4%	5.5%
1989	4.7%	5.3%
1990	4.1%	5.5%

Major Employment Sectors

Sector	Jobs	Market Share	Average Pay	5-Year Trend
Services	79,000	25%	$19,089	Warm
Wholesale and retail trade	77,100	24%	$11,368	Hot
Government	53,600	17%	$24,901	Cool
Manufacturing	51,800	16%	$30,861	Cold
Finance, insurance, and real estate	20,600	6%	$23,797	Cool
Transportation and utilities	19,500	6%	n.a.	Hot
Construction	15,600	5%	$26,701	Cold

TAMPA

Total Points: 634
Overall Grade: B+
National Rank: 9 of 73
Regional Rank: 5 of 28 (South)

Metro Area Report Card

Category	Points	Grade
Economic Momentum	61	B
Future Growth	65	B
Job Opportunities	66	B
Business Opportunities	58	B
Real Estate Opportunities	80	B
Equality of Opportunities	47	B
Overall	634	B+

Growth Potential of Metro Area Counties

Rank	County	Population	Per Capita Income	Growth Potential Points	Growth Potential Grade
1.	Hernando	101,115	$12,676	81	A+
2.	Pasco	281,131	$13,710	72	A
3.	Hillsborough	834,054	$16,044	53	B
4.	Pinellas	851,659	$21,255	32	C–

Entire metro area is in Florida.

Biggest Cities

City	County	Median House Price	Population
Tampa	Hillsborough	$59,000	280,015
Saint Petersburg	Pinellas	$63,000	238,629
Clearwater	Pinellas	$82,100	98,784
Largo	Pinellas	$71,500	65,674
Town 'n' Country*	Hillsborough	$74,300	60,946
Brandon*	Hillsborough	$84,800	57,985
Palm Harbor*	Pinellas	$97,400	50,256
Pinellas Park	Pinellas	$61,900	43,426
Dunedin	Pinellas	$76,500	34,012
Spring Hill*	Hernando	$68,000	31,117

*Census Designated Places. All others are incorporated communities.

Annual Unemployment Rates

Year	Metro Area	National
1985	5.0%	7.2%
1986	5.1%	7.0%
1987	4.8%	6.2%
1988	4.6%	5.5%
1989	5.0%	5.3%
1990	5.1%	5.5%

314

Major Employment Sectors

Sector	Jobs	Market Share	Average Pay	5-Year Trend
Services	276,500	31%	$18,888	Hot
Wholesale and retail trade	243,300	28%	$11,987	Hot
Government	114,900	13%	$23,188	Hot
Manufacturing	92,600	10%	$22,912	Cool
Finance, insurance, and real estate	64,900	7%	$22,993	Warm
Construction	49,600	6%	$20,424	Cold
Transportation and utilities	41,600	5%	n.a.	Hot

TOLEDO

Total Points: 426
Overall Grade: C–
National Rank: 58 of 73
Regional Rank: 9 of 14 (Midwest)

Metro Area Report Card

Category	Points	Grade
Economic Momentum	31	D
Future Growth	47	C–
Job Opportunities	38	D+
Business Opportunities	48	C
Real Estate Opportunities	82	B
Equality of Opportunities	12	D–
Overall	426	C–

Growth Potential of Metro Area Counties

Rank	County	Population	Per Capita Income	Growth Potential Points	Grade
1.	Wood	113,269	$16,742	34	C
2.	Fulton	38,498	$15,977	26	D
3.	Lucas	462,361	$17,005	24	D

Entire metro area is in Ohio.

Biggest Cities

City	County	Median House Price	Population
Toledo	Lucas	$48,900	332,943
Bowling Green	Wood	$81,700	28,176
Oregon	Lucas	$72,300	18,334

Annual Unemployment Rates

Year	Metro Area	National
1985	8.2%	7.2%
1986	8.4%	7.0%
1987	7.3%	6.2%
1988	5.9%	5.5%
1989	6.0%	5.3%
1990	6.9%	5.5%

Major Employment Sectors

Sector	Jobs	Market Share	Average Pay	5-Year Trend
Services	76,600	26%	$18,398	Hot
Wholesale and retail trade	72,100	25%	$10,599	Warm
Manufacturing	59,200	20%	$33,902	Cold
Government	43,900	15%	$24,599	Cool
Transportation and utilities	14,800	5%	n.a.	Cool
Finance, insurance, and real estate	12,100	4%	$22,246	Warm
Construction	11,800	4%	$28,843	Hot

TUCSON

Total Points: 558
Overall Grade: B–
National Rank: 24 of 73
Regional Rank: 9 of 14 (West)

Metro Area Report Card

Category	Points	Grade
Economic Momentum	45	C
Future Growth	84	A
Job Opportunities	49	C
Business Opportunities	44	C
Real Estate Opportunities	64	C
Equality of Opportunities	33	C
Overall	558	B–

Growth Potential of Metro Area County

County	Population	Per Capita Income	Growth Potential Points	Grade
Pima	666,880	$15,203	42	C+

Entire metro area is in Arizona.

Biggest Cities

City	County	Median House Price	Population
Tucson	Pima	$66,800	405,390
Flowing Wells*	Pima	$61,500	14,013
Green Valley*	Pima	$84,600	13,231

*Census Designated Places. All others are incorporated communities.

Annual Unemployment Rates

Year	Metro Area	National
1985	5.3%	7.2%
1986	5.7%	7.0%
1987	5.1%	6.2%
1988	5.1%	5.5%
1989	4.5%	5.3%
1990	4.1%	5.5%

Major Employment Sectors

Sector	Jobs	Market Share	Average Pay	5-Year Trend
Services	74,000	29%	$17,615	Hot
Wholesale and retail trade	60,200	24%	$11,404	Hot
Government	55,100	22%	$22,533	Warm
Manufacturing	26,500	10%	$31,353	Cold
Construction	14,700	6%	$19,950	Cold
Finance, insurance, and real estate	11,700	5%	$20,178	Cold
Transportation and utilities	9,500	4%	n.a.	Cold

TULSA

Total Points: 533
Overall Grade: C+
National Rank: 27 of 73
Regional Rank: 14 of 28 (South)

Metro Area Report Card

Category	Points	Grade
Economic Momentum	21	F
Future Growth	67	B
Job Opportunities	31	D–
Business Opportunities	57	B
Real Estate Opportunities	88	A–
Equality of Opportunities	55	B
Overall	533	C+

Growth Potential of Metro Area Counties

Rank	County	Population	Per Capita Income	Growth Potential Points	Grade
1.	Wagoner	47,883	$12,527	32	C–
2.	Rogers	55,170	$13,380	30	C–
3.	Tulsa	503,341	$17,289	28	D
4.	Creek	60,915	$13,484	26	D
5.	Osage	41,645	$11,469	19	F

Entire metro area is in Oklahoma.

Biggest Cities

City	County	Median House Price	Population
Tulsa	Tulsa	$60,500	367,302
Broken Arrow	Tulsa	$67,700	58,043
Sapulpa	Creek	$45,800	18,074

Annual Unemployment Rates

Year	Metro Area	National
1985	7.3%	7.2%
1986	8.5%	7.0%
1987	8.2%	6.2%
1988	7.3%	5.5%
1989	5.8%	5.3%
1990	5.3%	5.5%

Major Employment Sectors

Sector	Jobs	Market Share	Average Pay	5-Year Trend
Services	82,700	26%	$18,855	Warm
Wholesale and retail trade	74,000	23%	$11,769	Cold
Manufacturing	56,600	18%	$27,536	Warm
Government	38,700	12%	$19,753	Cool
Transportation and utilities	25,600	8%	n.a.	Hot
Finance, insurance, and real estate	17,600	6%	$23,840	Cold
Construction	11,700	4%	$22,022	Cold

WASHINGTON, D.C.

Total Points: 585
Overall Grade: B
National Rank: 17 of 73
Regional Rank: 1 of 17 (East)

Metro Area Report Card

Category	Points	Grade
Economic Momentum	57	B
Future Growth	47	C–
Job Opportunities	71	B+
Business Opportunities	60	B
Real Estate Opportunities	41	D+
Equality of Opportunities	66	A–
Overall	585	B

Growth Potential of Metro Area Counties

Rank	County	Population	Per Capita Income	Growth Potential Points	Growth Potential Grade
1.	Loudoun, Va.	86,129	$25,642	74	A
2.	Stafford, Va.	61,236	$19,267	72	A
3.	Calvert, Md.*	51,372	$20,277	69	A
	Prince William, Va.*	215,686	$20,278§	69	A
5.	Manassas, Va.†	27,957	$20,278§	61	A–
6.	Charles, Md.	101,154	$18,500	59	B+
7.	Frederick, Md.	150,208	$19,230	57	B+
8.	Montgomery, Md.*	757,027	$29,639	47	B
	Fairfax County, Va.*	818,584	$28,366§	47	B
10.	Prince George's, Md.	729,268	$18,960	37	C
11.	Arlington, Va.	170,936	$33,039	30	C–
12.	Alexandria, Va.†*	111,183	$31,264	28	D
	Manassas Park, Va.†*	6,734	$20,278§	28	D
14.	Fairfax city, Va.†	19,622	$28,366§	24	D
15.	Falls Church, Va.†	9,578	$28,366§	23	D
16.	Washington†	606,900	$22,998	17	F

*Tied in rank.
†Independent cities.
§The U.S. Bureau of Economic Analysis combines small independent cities with adjacent cities or counties for the purposes of calculating per capita income. Fairfax County, Fairfax city, and Falls Church formed a single unit for the income study, as did Prince William County, Manassas, and Manassas Park.
Counties are in the District of Columbia unless otherwise indicated.

Biggest Cities

City	County	Median House Price	Population
Washington	(independent city)	$123,900	606,900
Arlington, Va.*	Arlington	$231,000	170,936
Alexandria, Va.	(independent city)	$228,600	111,183
Silver Spring, Md.*	Montgomery	$179,900	76,046
Bethesda, Md.*	Montgomery	$327,200	62,936
Burke, Va.*	Fairfax	$201,300	57,734
Wheaton-Glenmont, Md.*	Montgomery	$155,400	53,720
Annandale, Va.*	Fairfax	$221,700	50,975
Reston, Va.*	Fairfax	$201,700	48,556
Dale City, Va.*	Prince William	$122,500	47,170

*Census Designated Places. All others are incorporated communities.
Cities are in the District of Columbia unless otherwise indicated.

Annual Unemployment Rates

Year	Metro Area	National
1985	3.7%	7.2%
1986	3.5%	7.0%
1987	3.2%	6.2%
1988	2.9%	5.5%
1989	2.7%	5.3%
1990	3.4%	5.5%

Major Employment Sectors

Sector	Jobs	Market Share	Average Pay	5-Year Trend
Services	756,500	34%	$27,980	Hot
Government	586,200	26%	$32,912	Cold
Wholesale and retail trade	434,300	19%	$15,325	Hot
Construction	136,200	6%	$27,509	Hot
Finance, insurance, and real estate	131,000	6%	$29,817	Hot
Transportation and utilities	108,000	5%	n.a.	Hot
Manufacturing	87,600	4%	$33,631	Hot

WEST PALM BEACH

Total Points: 820
Overall Grade: A+
National Rank: 1 of 73
Regional Rank: 1 of 28 (South)

Metro Area Report Card

Category	Points	Grade
Economic Momentum	83	A
Future Growth	88	A
Job Opportunities	67	B
Business Opportunities	98	A+
Real Estate Opportunities	54	C–
Equality of Opportunities	63	B+
Overall	820	A+

Growth Potential of Metro Area Counties

County	Population	Per Capita Income	Growth Potential Points	Growth Potential Grade
Palm Beach	863,518	$24,319	69	A

Entire metro area is in Florida.

Biggest Cities

City	County	Median House Price	Population
West Palm Beach	Palm Beach	$72,000	67,643
Boca Raton	Palm Beach	$165,300	61,492
Delray Beach	Palm Beach	$92,900	47,181
Boynton Beach	Palm Beach	$79,400	46,194
Lake Worth	Palm Beach	$66,900	28,564
Riviera Beach	Palm Beach	$61,600	27,639
Jupiter	Palm Beach	$111,500	24,986
Palm Beach Gardens	Palm Beach	$137,700	22,965
Wellington*	Palm Beach	$145,700	20,670

*Census Designated Place. All others are incorporated communities.

Annual Unemployment Rates

Year	Metro Area	National
1985	6.2%	7.2%
1986	5.9%	7.0%
1987	5.4%	6.2%
1988	5.0%	5.5%
1989	6.0%	5.3%
1990	6.5%	5.5%

Major Employment Sectors

Sector	Jobs	Market Share	Average Pay	5-Year Trend
Services	116,200	32%	$21,557	Hot
Wholesale and retail trade	96,600	27%	$13,579	Hot
Government	46,500	13%	$24,221	Hot
Manufacturing	33,100	9%	$34,711	Cold
Finance, insurance, and real estate	28,700	8%	$28,749	Hot
Construction	25,600	7%	$23,478	Cold
Transportation and utilities	14,500	4%	n.a.	Hot